TRUE LEADERSHIP

How to Become the Type of Leader
People Want to Follow

**Unlocking the Secrets of
Authentic Leadership for
Maximum Influence and Impact**

DR GABRIEL BOLU

True Leadership: How to Become the Type of Leader People Want to Follow
© Copyright 2023. Dr Gabriel Nnamdi Bolu

All rights reserved. No part of this publication may be reproduced, distributed, or transmitted in any form or by any means, including photocopying, recording, or other electronic or mechanical methods, without the prior written permission of the publisher, except in the case of brief quotations embodied in critical reviews and certain other non-commercial uses permitted by copyright law.

Although the author and publisher have tried to ensure that the information in this book was correct at press time, the author and publisher do not assume and hereby disclaim any liability to any party for any loss, damage, or disruption caused by errors or omissions, whether such errors or omissions result from negligence, accident, or any other cause.

Adherence to all applicable laws and regulations, including international, federal, state, and local governing laws, professional business practices, advertising, and all other aspects of doing business in the United States (US), Canada, or any other jurisdiction, is the sole responsibility of the reader and consumer.

Neither the author nor the publisher assume any responsibility or liability whatsoever on behalf of the consumer or reader of this material. Any perceived slight of any individual or organisation is unintentional.

The resources in this book are provided for informational purposes only and should not be used to replace the specialised training and judgement of a health care or mental health care professional.

Neither the author nor the publisher can be held responsible for the use of the information provided within this book. Please always consult a trained professional before deciding regarding the treatment of yourself or others.

For more information, email nnamdi11@hotmail.com

ISBN: 979-8-89109-189-4 - paperback
ISBN: 979-8-89109-192-4 - ebook

Table of Contents

FOREWORD v
DEDICATION ix
INTRODUCTION. xi

PART ONE: The Foundation of Great Leadership: Values and Vision

CHAPTER 1: Leaders Inspire Change Through Vision . . .1

CHAPTER 2: Leaders Develop Other Leaders. 15

CHAPTER 3: Character is Key to Leadership 31

PART TWO: Understanding Leadership: Principles, Qualities, and Practices

CHAPTER 4: Defining Leadership:
 Perspectives and Insights. 43

CHAPTER 5: Five Key Principles I Have
 Learned About Leadership 67

CHAPTER 6: The Type of Leader People Want to Follow:
 Traits and Qualities. 85

PART THREE: Becoming That Leader and Valuing It Once You Are

CHAPTER 7: Three Steps to Becoming a
 Leader People Want to Follow. 99

CHAPTER 8: The Benefits and Price of Becoming the
        Type of Leader People Want to Follow . .131

CHAPTER 9: The Power and Benefit of Gratitude 143

EPILOGUE. 161
CALL TO ACTION 161
ACKNOWLEDGEMENTS .165
ABOUT THE AUTHOR 167

Foreword

"The privilege of a lifetime is to become who you truly are."
- Dr Carl Jung

The works of Homer, Livy, Shakespeare, Tolstoy, Mantel, and others. The canon of our world's great religions. The political stratagems of Machiavelli and Sun Tzu. Narrations concerning the lives of seminal personalities across the rivers of time. Contemporary management literature. Whether implied or explicitly stated, these disparate bodies of work and schools of thought – spanning the breadth of theology, geopolitics, literature, economics, history, and warfare – are all suffused with the import of leadership.

Indeed, the entire corpus of world history summates to a confluence of narrative threads wherein the fortunes, and times, of entire peoples and civilisations typically distils to and/or becomes synonymous with the actions (benign or malignant) of a few consequential characters. Whether germane to view history as materially contingent on the provincial actions of a cohort of key leading figures (paraphrasing Tolstoy *"Does the vast herd really move by the action of one? Or rather is there some nebulous shared consciousness guiding the current of the herd?")* is not the point. What is salient is that we typically (and reflexively) process, interpret and understand history, as well as our modern world, through the lens of leadership.

In the freedoms, rights, opportunities, and economic welfare of peoples (as well as corporations and nation states) we see the spectre of leadership as a principal operative force in either the suppression or maximisation of these domains.

From the fall of Rome ... to the Allies stand against the Third Reich and the Axis Powers ... to the launch of the iPhone ... to the collapse of Lehman Brothers and the ensuing global financial crisis. All adduce varying degrees of either desirable or pathological (in some cases tyrannical) leadership.

It is for these reasons - i.e., the criticality of leadership in achieving desired outcomes across diverse domains – that we as people are rightly concerned with examining, dissecting, explicating, and attempting to formularise (and ultimately master) the subject. The evidence for this can be seen in the plethora of business, personal development, self-help, and other such books which tackle the issue. Successfully so in some cases - less successfully in others.

With *True Leadership*, Dr Gabriel Bolu makes a deeply personal, unique, and triumphant contribution to the canon of works. With disarming probity, clarity of thought, and elegant parsimony in prose, Dr Bolu systematically lays out the framework and process by which one might transmute into the type of leader people want to follow.

Foreword

The verb "*transmute*" proves apt, as the centrality of Dr Bolu's claims rests on his belief (expertly argued and communicated) that true leadership is founded upon the cornerstone of *personal leadership* - itself the product of transformation through intentional self-discovery. Weaving together a veritable tapestry of real-world examples, management theories, exercises and, not least, his own remarkable professional and personal evolution, Dr Bolu paints a striking portrait for us. When one steps back from the iridescent piece it is clear - as Dr Bolu intends it to be - that character and empathy are the primary colours which animate the canvass.

This focus on personal leadership (i.e., intentional self-discovery and the cultivation of personal character – consisting of empathy, service, and gratitude) is what really makes Dr Bolu's leadership thesis truly unique.

Whether you are currently a leader, or aspire to leadership, or are like countless individuals who – via the vicissitudes of life - finds themselves unexpectedly confronted with the challenge(s) of leadership … this heartwarming, and life affirming, discourse is written for you.

Indeed, *True Leadership's* economy, humanity, and applicability make it a manuscript that one can easily (and must) return to again, and again. For its deeper truth lies in the revelation of your best personal self … the perennial foundation of true leadership.

May this honest and beautifully written exposition inspire you as it has me.

Dr Michael Arumemi-Ikhide

DEDICATION

I would like to dedicate this book to my two most important mentors: my father, Professor Christian Bolu, and the late Dr Myles Munroe. You both have had a significant influence on the person I have become. I'll be forever grateful. Thank you.

Introduction

Unexpected Circumstances, Extraordinary Leadership

I start this literary journey by exploring the remarkable stories of two individuals in unexpected situations. The first story is about Volodymyr Zelenskyy, who became the president of Ukraine after a comedy and television production career. The second story is my personal journey, where I found myself thrust into a prime leadership role without the expected experience. These stories illustrate how leadership is tested in unexpected situations.

These stories set the stage for the chapters that follow. We will explore the foundations, principles, and practices of authentic leadership. We lay a strong groundwork for your own leadership journey by delving into the power of vision, how leaders develop other leaders, and the importance of cultivating character.

True Leadership

Volodymyr Zelenskyy's Story

Volodymyr Zelenskyy, the president of Ukraine, had always been a man of humble origins and unexpected successes. From a comedian and television producer, he rose to the highest office in his country through a landslide victory in the presidential election. However, even in his wildest dreams, he never imagined the immense challenges and tests of leadership that awaited him.

Ukraine had been recovering from years of political instability and economic struggles. Zelenskyy focused on implementing reforms, fighting corruption, and improving the lives of his citizens. He was determined to bring about positive change and build a prosperous future for Ukraine.

Zelenskyy's peace and progress was ended by Russian president Vladimir Putin's invasion. The attack caught the world by surprise. Zelenskyy faced an unparalleled crisis that demanded all his leadership skills.

Zelenskyy was thrust into the unknown. He had to become a wartime president. He had to command the respect of his army and garner the support of his people. This is a challenging leadership position that few would take.

With his country under siege, Zelenskyy rallied his people, uniting them against the common threat. He displayed immense resilience and determination, refusing to succumb to fear or despair. Addressing the nation, he called for unity and urged his fellow citizens to stand strong in the face of aggression. Zelenskyy's ability to connect with people on a

Introduction

personal level became an invaluable asset as he sought international support.

Zelenskyy's leadership during the invasion earned him respect both at home and abroad. His commitment to his people was unwavering. He showed his ability to make tough decisions. His determination to protect Ukraine's sovereignty earned him worldwide admiration. He became a symbol of resilience and a voice for the Ukrainian people in their struggle against aggression.

> Volodymyr Zelenskyy's story is one of unexpected circumstances and extraordinary leadership. From a comedian to a president facing an invasion he rose to the occasion, demonstrating courage, resilience, and strategic acumen. His ability to rally his people, gain international support, and manage a complex crisis left a lasting impact on Ukraine's history and people. This illustrated his leadership capacity and ability.

My Story

I had a similar experience landing a prime leadership position without the experience. It was a dream job. Despite my excitement, I was anxious about performing well in the role since I lacked experience. I felt like an imposter. I worried about being exposed shortly after starting the job.

The year started off great for me. My wife and I had a new baby. I had completed my PhD after four long years. I had just turned thirty as well. After six months of looking for a job, I landed one beyond my wildest dreams. I was going to be part of the executive team of an international company. I would be the head of Corporate and Business Strategy, reporting to the CEO. This was my dream job. It was a job that matched my strengths and ambitions.

I always had a passion for leadership. I had spent the last twelve years studying leadership and learning from great mentors, including my father. So, when I got this job, I thought I had arrived at my destiny. However, I never thought I would get the job at the tender age of thirty. I had barely started my working career.

The reality of the expectations of the role became clear to me within the first couple of weeks. My total lack of experience in the role became apparent. I had no industry experience. I was expected to create and implement the business strategy for the CEO and the board of directors. This was daunting for me.

I had no direct experience in influencing people at the highest level in a corporate organisation. I had never been in a senior management role. Yet, I had to command the respect of all the various direct reports of the CEO, including the CFO, CCO, and various other executives. These senior executives saw I had no industry or senior management experience. I was in a very vulnerable position. All I had was the CEO's confidence. The CEO handpicking me for this role showed great confidence in me.

I felt like a fake and exposed. But while I had insecurities, I still believed I could be successful. I had very little time to figure out what type of leader I was going to be. How would I get these seasoned executives to listen to me and buy into my ideas? What type of leadership style would I employ? This was the real deal, not theoretical anymore. I knew I had to perform well or I was done. I may have a few months of grace, but my role was critical to the company, so the CEO would not hesitate to do what was right for his firm.

I also had my personal life on the line. I had moved my young family across the country for this role, hoping to be successful enough to support them. Thankfully, it all turned out well. I made a success of the role and won the respect and admiration of my CEO and peers.

The stories emphasise the importance of leadership skills for personal and professional success. Leadership development has become a hot topic as businesses and organisations recognise its importance for their success and continued growth.

This book offers practical strategies and insights to develop leadership skills for thriving in today's complex world. You will lay a strong foundation for your leadership journey by exploring the power of vision, developing other leaders, cultivating character, and more.

This book will empower you to become the type of leader people want to follow. It will show you how to inspire change and build relationships with resilience and integrity. Each chapter provides actionable advice, exercises, and examples to help you lead.

Part One, *The Foundation of Great Leadership: Values and Vision,* lays the groundwork for your leadership journey. It explores the power of vision, the importance of developing other leaders, and the significance of character in leadership.

Part Two, *Understanding Leadership: Principles and Practices,* delves deeper into the essence of leadership. It examines various definitions and perspectives of leadership. We'll share key principles learned from experience. It explains qualities of inspiring leaders and provides guidance for becoming a leader people want to follow.

Part Three, *Becoming That Leader and Valuing It Once You Are,* outlines the three steps to becoming the type of leader people want to follow. We uncover the true essence of becoming an authentic leader destined to fulfil and maximise their leadership potential. This section also uncovers the personal aspects of leadership, exploring the costs and rewards of leadership. Finally, we highlight the importance of gratitude and thankfulness in leadership.

Each chapter expands your knowledge, challenges your assumptions, and inspires you to take intentional steps toward becoming the true leader you are.

Start your journey of self-discovery and leadership growth now. Together, let us uncover the secrets of authentic leadership and unleash the power within you to become the type of leader people want to follow.

Your leadership story is waiting to be written. Let's begin.

PART ONE

The Foundation of Great Leadership: Values and Vision

CHAPTER 1

Leaders Inspire Change Through Vision

There is nothing permanent except change.
~ Heraclitus

The Power of Vision and Change

Change is an inevitable and constant factor that permeates all aspects of our lives. It is a pivotal element within our personal, professional, and societal lives, shaping our experiences and moulding our futures. From the gentle progression of seasons to unexpected life events, change presents both opportunities and challenges. Leaders understand the benefits and challenges that change brings and embrace it as agents of transformation.

Leadership is not about maintaining the status quo, but about initiating and driving change. Vision plays a central role in this process, as leaders create a compelling picture of a preferred future and articulate it passionately. Vision represents the journey from the current state to a better tomorrow. It inspires people to think beyond their current circumstances, encouraging them to dream big.

A vision alone is not enough. Leaders must secure support from their teams to make change happen. They understand that change requires the collective effort of people who are affected by it. Proactive communication, addressing issues, and understanding the benefits are key to overcoming opposition and driving change.

This chapter explores the power of vision and change. It showcases examples of leaders who have successfully initiated and advanced change in various contexts. Through these stories, we learn that vision is not static; it evolves, adapts, and remains relevant as circumstances change.

Greta Thunberg's Story

Meet Greta Thunberg, a prominent climate change activist who reached the age of twenty in January 2023. She has encouraged students and leaders worldwide to recognise the environmental harm being caused by governments and businesses. Thunberg gained international attention through her school strike for climate action. Her activism began when she skipped school every Friday to sit outside the Swedish Parliament with a sign that read "School strike for climate." This action sparked a global movement known as Fridays for Future. It inspired students around the world to demand urgent action to address the climate crisis.

CHAPTER 1

In 2019, she delivered a powerful and inspiring speech at the UN Climate Action Summit, earning a rousing standing ovation. Thunberg showcased her leadership and ability to inspire change. She passionately explained why governments' current climate change policies are unacceptable. She presented a clear vision of the future for herself and her peers. Her speech and earlier protest in her home country have inspired many to act worldwide. Thunberg is resolute in advancing her clear vision, despite personal sacrifices.

Her activism has had a significant impact on her childhood. She missed out on a proper education and faced a lot of criticism. For instance, figures like former president Donald Trump have criticised her approach. Despite differing opinions, Thunberg's activism significantly mobilised young people and elevated the urgency of climate action on a global stage.

She continues to be a prominent voice in the fight against climate change and a symbol of youth-led activism for a sustainable future. Thunberg is fearless and determined to progress her vision, irrespective of opposition. Her passion for advancing her cause is a prime example of the power of vision and change.

Thunberg received TIME's Person of the Year award and earned a Nobel Peace Prize nomination in 2019. Such honours underscore the significance of her contributions and amplify her message to a global audience. Even as she gains recognition, her mission remains resolute. She aims to force the world to pay attention and act decisively on the pressing issue of climate change. The world watches as this young climate warrior continues her crucial mission.

The Premise

Change is inevitable and a constant in our lives.

Change is an inevitable and constant factor permeating all aspects of our lives. It is a pivotal element within our personal, professional, and societal lives, one that continues to shape our experiences and mould our futures.

Change embodies transitioning from one state, situation, or condition to another. It can be as subtle as the gentle progression of seasons or as jarring as an unexpected life event. Nonetheless, change always presents both opportunities and challenges.

We can witness the traces of change in the mirror each day. Every wrinkle and grey hair is a testament to time's transformative power. Likewise, in its constant state of evolution, society shows the marks of change. In the crucible of societal discourse, old norms are challenged, perspectives shift, and values are redefined.

Similarly, in the realm of commerce, change is the driving force that propels industries forward. Businesses adapt, innovate, and reinvent themselves to stay competitive.

Change is all around us. It's woven into our reality, influencing everything from history to daily routines. Yet, despite its ubiquity and inevitability, many of us are resistant to its pull. Change disrupts the status quo and shatters the comfort of familiar routines, which can be unsettling. We often seek the solace of predictability, forgetting that adaptability and resilience are keys to survival.

We would do well to remember that every sunrise is a herald of change, reminding us of the unending cycle of life. Let's not just adapt to change, but embrace, learn, and grow from it.

Nothing improves without change.

Nothing improves without change. This truth manifests in every sphere of life and in every corner of the globe. Indeed, any progress we witness, whether in our personal lives or within our companies, stems directly from our willingness and ability to adapt and evolve.

One needs only to consider the technological revolution of the past few decades to appreciate the scale of change we've experienced. The remarkable advancements we've seen worldwide are a testament to this. From the internet to the proliferation of smartphones, change has been a powerful force driving innovation and improvement.

Take the evolution of mobile phones over the past twenty years as an example. These devices have altered our lives, redefined our means of communication, and transformed the way we manage our daily tasks. Today, I, like millions of others, conduct most of my commerce using my mobile phone. This minor change has made a tremendous impact, replacing the need for a wallet and making my purchases faster and more convenient.

Beyond the realm of technology, change can also have far-reaching effects on society. Consider the monumental changes inspired by civil rights leaders like Dr Martin Luther King Jr. in the 1960s. His unyielding demand for a change in the treatment of Black people in the United States spurred a radical shift in societal attitudes. While discrimination persists, civil rights for Black people have improved worldwide.

The reality of change is complex. It requires a careful balance of maintaining what works and challenging what doesn't. Discomfort is often a necessary precursor to improvement. The instances mentioned above underline the fact that nothing improves without change. They emphasize the significance of intentional and meaningful change that strives to improve rather than just being different.

Leaders are change agents.

Leaders understand the benefits of change and the challenges it brings, including opposition. Many people prefer their comfort zones and find change daunting. Leaders, however, stand apart. They do not wait for change to occur; instead, they instigate it. They embrace change and use it to their advantage. Leaders view change as an opportunity for growth.

McKinsey reports that 70 percent of company change programs fail because of employee resistance and lack of management support. Leadership, or lack thereof, plays a significant role in these failed transformations. It's a common tale: a significant change is announced, and excitement and communication are rampant for a few weeks. Once the excitement that started the change dissipates, the entire initiative fizzles out.

Microsoft's Story

Change is hard. It is often met with resistance. Yet, no company can survive, grow, or reach its potential without embracing change. Take Microsoft as an example.

Less than a decade ago, most of its Windows software was sold via CDs or preinstalled on desktops with a one-time fee. Today, Microsoft delivers its software through the cloud as a subscription-based service. Microsoft's leaders saw cloud computing coming and made the change. Microsoft is reaping the benefits of this transition. The Microsoft of today differs from the one Bill Gates founded several decades ago.

A leader cannot lead without initiating change. A leader's success or failure is often determined by their ability to start and/or manage change. George Bush's leadership legacy, for instance, was defined by the way he handled 9/11. He was transformed into a wartime president, similar to Abraham Lincoln, Franklin D. Roosevelt, and John F. Kennedy.

> *Those who look only to the past or present*
> *are certain to miss the future!*
> *- John F. Kennedy*

TRUE LEADERSHIP

Leaders inspire change through a vision of a preferred future.

In a *Harvard Business Review* (HBR) interview, legendary GE Chairman and CEO Jack Welch was asked, "What makes a good manager?" He responded, "I prefer the term 'business leader.' Good business leaders create a vision, articulate the vision, passionately own the vision, and relentlessly drive it to completion." This distinction illuminates the difference between a manager and a leader.

The terms *leader* and *vision* are often synonymous. The number one responsibility of any leader is to develop a vision. While most leaders can create that – either with their team or consultants' help – the best leaders also drive this vision to completion. A well-worded vision alone doesn't ensure its advancement. For a vision to come alive, the team must resonate with and buy into it.

Vision signifies change. It represents the journey from the current state to a preferred future – a shift that involves change. This is why vision is a critical aspect of leadership. Many change initiatives fail because of a lack of clear vision and strategy.

A compelling vision of the desired future state, coupled with a well-defined strategy, is crucial for successful change. Without clear direction, employees become confused about the change's purpose and expected outcomes. This leads to resistance, apathy, and disengagement.

A lack of vision can render companies stagnant, enabling competitors to surge ahead. It's a pattern we see repeatedly.

Progressive companies usually have a clear vision that employees support. Companies don't fail because of a lack of talent or ideas. Failure stems from no vision, or inaction on it.

Vision is about the future – a preferable future. Leaders guide people to destinations they haven't reached before. When Elon Musk started SpaceX, few believed in its potential. SpaceX was looking to do the impossible. Musk inspired people toward an unfamiliar goal, and some may say an impossible task.

Today, SpaceX's accomplishments seem plausible, but this wasn't the case when they embarked on the journey. Vision can inspire people to think beyond their current circumstances. This releases them from their limitations and encourages them to dream big. This is how individuals and companies achieve extraordinary things – and it all begins with a compelling vision.

Leaders drive change through people.

While leaders initiate change, they also inspire others to act and make change happen. Vision influences action. It compels people to move in a specific direction. That's why it's crucial for a leader to secure support from their team for their vision. It determines how people allocate their time, spend resources, hire personnel, and more. When a leader is infused with a vision, it's apparent and infectious. Conversely, when they lack a powerful vision, it's also evident.

Vision provides a sense of purpose and motivation. Knowing the organisation's larger objectives can lead to employees feeling more connected to their work. This is important in challenging times when team morale needs bolstering.

Great leaders advance their vision despite opposition. Every vision will be tested for legitimacy. If there is no opposition, then the vision may not be compelling enough. Opposition doesn't invalidate the vision. Great leaders understand how to persevere in the face of resistance. They know how to garner the support to execute their vision.

Leaders recognise that proactive and effective communication is crucial to overcoming opposition. They are open about the reasons for the proposed changes. These leaders address concerns proactively and ensure everyone understands the benefits of the new direction.

Make no mistake: vision is crucial in driving change through others. It is the paramount responsibility of a leader. Without a clear destination, a leader can't inspire people to enact change. A vision fosters cohesion within a company or a team. While individuals, teams, or groups have their own goals, they still require a collective vision from their leader.

Leaders understand that a vision is not a static idea. It needs to evolve as the company grows and as market conditions change. They continually reassess their vision and adjust it as needed. They ensure it remains compelling and relevant.

My Story

I led an exciting change program at my previous airline company which resulted in turning around a key operational performance area. It was a challenging initiative, but it was crucial for our survival.

In my role as Chief of Staff to the CEO, I was responsible for improving our poor on-time performance (OTP). Anyone familiar with the airline industry knows that OTP is one of the most critical metrics. Any airline with a poor OTP is in serious trouble, as customers dislike being delayed. Unfortunately, we had a poor record in this area, which was tarnishing our reputation. The CEO assigned me to find a solution and address the issue.

Everyone recognised the problem, but the causes were unclear. I devoted considerable time to uncovering the underlying issues. I discovered that the problem wasn't what most people assumed. The root causes cut across several departments and were within the control of the same staff who complained about the poor OTP. They were not looking at themselves hard enough. Resolving this problem required a radical change in how the operational team performed their duties. However, it was difficult to change how people worked, as employee morale was low.

Despite these challenges, I understood what was needed to solve the problem. My vision was to become the most punctual airline in the country. I believed it was achievable.

Gaining staff support required more than just sending an email and imposing changes. Instead, I immersed myself in the operational team, working alongside them for a period to identify the root cause together. Second, I encouraged them to articulate the root cause and propose solutions themselves.

They arrived at the same conclusion I did, and together, we crafted a solution and a shared vision.

We then had to execute our plan to deliver the vision, which was no simple task. Over six months, we experienced a dramatic increase in our on-time performance. Our customers were astonished and gave us unusual but well-deserved praise. We meticulously measured our performance and conducted weekly customer surveys to track improvement and maintain standards.

This initiative taught me the importance of team alignment, accountability, collaboration, and performance measurement. Most importantly, it showed me that change is best achieved through collaboration with the people who are directly impacted.

With my authority, I could have easily tried to force change, which might have yielded short-term results. Such an approach wouldn't have been sustainable, and could have damaged relationships and trust. By taking the path I did, I could deliver results while simultaneously building and enhancing relationships across the company.

ACTION PLAN

1. Write three changes you want to see in your personal life or at work. This will be a change you are going to start and advance to completion.
2. For each change, write the names of people the change will impact. It could either be yourself alone or include other people.

CHAPTER 1

3. For each change, write the situation's current state and the preferred future.
4. For each change, write why you want the change to happen and the benefit for you and others.
5. For each change, write the potential opposition from others.

_____
_____
_____
_____
_____
_____
_____
_____
_____
_____
_____
_____
_____
_____
_____
_____
_____
_____
_____
_____

Reflection and Looking Forward

In this chapter, we discussed how change is inevitable and constant in our lives. Without change, no improvement can occur. Leaders play a crucial role as change agents, inspiring and driving change by envisioning a desired future. This is one of the key responsibilities of leaders – it is not optional if they want to succeed.

To thrive as a leader, you must embrace change, initiate it, and see it through to completion. It is essential to have a clear vision of the desired change. Equally important is getting buy-in from others, especially those who will be affected by the change.

In the next chapter, we will explore another critical responsibility of leaders. It is a duty that cannot be delegated and should be a top priority for leaders: developing other leaders.

The best leaders understand the significance of creating opportunities for other leaders to grow and develop. They promote a culture of continuous learning, providing resources for growth. Autonomy allows individuals to develop self-confidence. Collaboration cultivates essential leadership qualities.

Leaders invest in mentoring and coaching, sharing knowledge and experience. Exceptional leaders help individuals reach their full potential and benefit the organisation. They create a culture of growth, development, and collective achievement.

CHAPTER 2

LEADERS DEVELOP OTHER LEADERS

Great leaders create more leaders, not followers.
~ Roy T. Bennett

Developing Leaders from Within

True leadership extends beyond individual accomplishments and focuses on developing others. It is not enough for leaders to lead. They must also invest in nurturing and developing other leaders within their organisation. This chapter focuses on leaders developing other leaders to achieve organisational success.

Investing in other leaders increases impact and spreads decision-making. Empowering others promotes organisational expansion. When leaders create more leaders, they tap into the full potential of the entire team. This enables the organisation to achieve its goals more effectively.

We'll explore how leaders develop other leaders in this chapter. We will delve into the strategies, benefits, and best practices employed by exceptional leaders and top-performing companies.

Indra Nooyi's Story

Former CEO of PepsiCo, Indra Nooyi, is recognised for her efforts to cultivate leadership within PepsiCo. Indra understood the importance of cultivating leaders for the company's long-term success. Her vision was a program to foster collaboration, innovation, and diversity.

To bring her vision to life, Indra spearheaded the creation of various initiatives and programs at PepsiCo. One of her key endeavours was establishing the PepsiCo Leadership Academy. This academy provided comprehensive training for all employees.

The PepsiCo Leadership Academy provided workshops, seminars, and online courses. These programs included strategic thinking, communication, financial acumen, and problem-solving. Indra believed teaching employees these skills would make them better leaders and drive growth and innovation.

Indra recognised the significance of mentorship and coaching in leadership development. She urged executives to mentor promising talent. Seasoned professionals can provide invaluable insights, guidance, and support through one-on-one coaching sessions. This program helped people progress in their careers and understand PepsiCo's values and strategies.

Indra implemented a unique leadership approach by pushing her employees to take risks and face new challenges. She believed that the best leaders are those who will step outside their comfort zones and learn from both successes and failures. Indra fostered an atmosphere of exploration and experimentation.

Under Indra's leadership, PepsiCo thrived not only as a business, but also as a breeding ground for exceptional leaders. The company witnessed a steady influx of talent rising through the ranks, equipped with the skills, knowledge, and mindset to drive PepsiCo's continued success in the ever-evolving marketplace.

Indra Nooyi's dedication to leadership development made PepsiCo renowned for its leaders. Her vision and initiatives created a legacy of leadership excellence that inspires PepsiCo today.

The Premise

Leaders need to focus on developing other leaders.

Leaders can expand their impact by nurturing and developing other leaders.

You need a team of leaders to achieve significant results.

To achieve significant results, a leader needs a team of leaders. It takes a collective of leaders working together to accomplish remarkable outcomes. Reproducing and developing other leaders is not optional; it is critical for the survival and success of the organisation.

By investing in the development of other leaders, those in leadership positions can scale their impact. They can delegate responsibilities and give others leadership roles, helping the organisation expand. Creating more leaders allows the organisation to reach its goals more effectively.

Building a team of leaders goes beyond relying on the abilities of one individual. It acknowledges the power of collaboration and recognises that shared leadership strengthens the organisation. Leaders can use the unique talents and expertise of others to benefit the organisation by developing them. This approach maximises collective potential and enhances problem-solving.

Having a team of leaders allows for better adaptability and resilience. Multiple leaders and perspectives keep the organisation agile. A team of leaders can navigate challenges, seize opportunities, and make informed decisions that consider a wide range of factors. It distributes responsibility, lessens risks, and builds a more reliable leadership structure.

The importance of developing other leaders can't be overstated. Leaders are essential for growth and significant results.

Develop other leaders for long-term success.

Developing other leaders is crucial for sustaining long-term success. No leader remains in the same role forever. Every leader, irrespective of their level within the organisation, should focus on developing other leaders.

By developing other leaders, organisations ensure their long-term success and sustainability. Mentoring and nurturing others enables leaders to develop a pool of potential leaders. This approach ensures continuity and prevents a leadership vacuum during times of transition or change.

Developing other leaders contributes to building a resilient and adaptable organisation. Nurturing new leaders creates an environment of learning, growth, and adaptation. This culture enables the organisation to navigate challenges, changes, and uncertainties more effectively. Multiple leaders enable the organisation to adjust to various situations without relying on individuals.

No single leader has all the answers.

In today's world, no single leader possesses all the answers. To operate effectively, organisations must embrace a team-based approach to decision-making. A team of capable leaders ensures that the best decisions are made and that collective responsibility is fostered.

Cultivating other leaders encourages distributed decision-making within an organisation. Instead of relying on a single leader to make all the decisions, multiple leaders can share the responsibility. This allows for diverse perspectives and expertise in decision-making, easing the burden on the primary leader. As a result, decisions become more well-rounded and informed.

Great leaders are intentional about developing leaders.

Great leaders understand the importance of intentionally developing other leaders. They recognise that cultivating leadership abilities in others benefits individuals and the organisation's success. These leaders are proactive in identifying and investing in the potential of their team members, providing them with opportunities for growth, learning, and skills development.

Intentional leadership development involves a strategic approach. Great leaders assess the strengths, weaknesses, and potential of individuals in their teams. They find areas for improvement and develop plans that fit the organisation and individual. They offer valuable feedback to help individuals improve their leadership skills.

Intentional leaders create a culture that values leadership development. They encourage individuals to take on new challenges and responsibilities. They equip their team members with resources, training, and networking to hone their leadership skills.

Great leaders also lead by example. They demonstrate the behaviours and qualities they want to see in other leaders, serving as role models and inspiration. They promote open communication, trust, and collaboration. This creates a secure space for individuals to express ideas, take risks, and learn from both successes and failures.

Intentional leadership development strengthens the talent pipeline and creates a legacy of effectiveness. These leaders recognise the benefits of investing in others, both for the individuals and the organisation.

Great leaders recognise the significance of intentionally developing other leaders. They take a proactive approach to identifying, nurturing, and supporting the potential of their team members, creating a culture that values leadership development. They strive to build a solid leadership pipeline to guarantee the success of their organisation.

Leaders understand the importance of recruiting well.

Leaders understand the criticality of effective recruiting practices. They recognise that to develop the best leaders, the process begins with recruiting the right individuals. While this may seem like an obvious concept but it is not always executed, often because of two key reasons.

Leaders may struggle to find the right candidates without an understanding of effective leadership. It is imperative to have a well-defined picture and a comprehension of what good leadership entails. Leaders lacking strong leadership qualities will struggle to find exceptional leaders.

Leaders attract candidates similar to themselves. People are drawn to those who share similar qualities. Recruiting exceptional leaders requires looking for candidates with qualities and skills. Leaders can spot leadership qualities in others. Leaders lacking these qualities will struggle to recruit excellent leaders.

Leaders understand that recruiting well is a fundamental aspect of developing exceptional leaders. They understand the importance of strong leadership and aim to live up to those standards. Leaders must look beyond biases to attract and develop top-tier leaders.

Leaders develop other leaders by empowering them and holding them accountable.

Leadership development involves empowering individuals and holding them accountable. The best leaders understand that creating other leaders goes beyond imparting knowledge and skills. It encourages individuals to reach their leadership potential.

Level 4 and 5 leaders excel in empowering people to lead. Once they have identified capable leaders, they provide them with the freedom to exercise their leadership abilities. However, this empowerment is not without accountability. Leaders understand the importance of clear expectations, metrics, and accountability. Leaders foster an environment of accountability to help individuals succeed.

Empowerment stems from trust and a sense of security. Leaders must trust their team members, even if they approach tasks or challenges differently. Insecure leaders may struggle to empower others, especially if they fear being overshadowed by those who can perform better.

The best leaders understand the importance of recruiting individuals better than themselves. They seek individuals who can surpass their own abilities, and once recruited, they empower them to excel. Level 4 and 5 leaders are secure individuals who prioritise the success and value of others, putting their team's needs before their own.

Developing other leaders empowers individuals and fosters their personal and professional growth. Developing team members enhances their skills, expands their knowledge, and gives them new challenges. This benefits the organisation and furthers individual team members. These developmental opportunities create a positive and thriving work environment.

Leaders empower individuals and hold them accountable. Leaders create an environment where individuals can flourish by providing freedom, trust, and support. Maintaining accountability benefits both the organisation and individual.

The best leaders create opportunities for other leaders to grow and develop.

The best leaders understand the significance of creating opportunities for other leaders to grow and develop. Nurturing leadership requires delegation, learning, autonomy, collaboration, and development.

Delegation is a crucial aspect of leadership development. Leaders give team members decision-making and initiative-leading opportunities. By delegating authority, leaders develop leadership skills and instil a sense of pride and accountability in others.

Creating a culture of continuous learning is another hallmark of exceptional leaders. They encourage team members to seek new knowledge, acquire new skills, and pursue personal and professional growth. These leaders create a learning environment through workshops, conferences, and other developmental opportunities.

Effective leaders also foster an environment that allows individuals to be autonomous and independent in their work. Leaders offer help, and trust their team members to make decisions and take ownership. By promoting autonomy, leaders empower individuals to develop self-confidence and become leaders.

Great leaders emphasise the value of collaboration and teamwork. Leadership is about collective effort, not individual achievement. These leaders create chances for people to work together and build a cooperative culture. Leaders promote teamwork to develop communication, collaboration, and conflict resolution.

Leaders invest in their team through mentoring and coaching. They provide constructive feedback to help individuals improve their leadership skills. By serving as mentors, they inspire and empower others to embrace leadership roles.

In summary, the best leaders recognise the importance of creating opportunities for other leaders to grow and develop. Delegation, learning, autonomy, collaboration, development, and mentoring are all prioritised to cultivate leadership potential. They help the organisation succeed long term by supporting and empowering other leaders.

CHAPTER 2
Great leaders create a culture of trust.

Trust is a critical element in developing leaders. Great leaders understand the importance of creating a culture of trust within their teams and organisations. They recognise that trust forms the foundation for strong relationships, effective collaboration, and personal growth.

Great leaders lead by example and show trustworthiness. They act with integrity and keep their commitments. This consistency builds trust among team members.

Great leaders encourage open and honest communication. They create an environment where individuals feel safe to express their ideas, share their concerns, and provide feedback. They listen to their team members, value their perspectives, and ensure that everyone's voice is heard. Openness builds trust and encourages participation.

Leaders empower their team members by delegating responsibilities and providing autonomy. Leaders show trust in their capabilities by giving individuals the freedom to make decisions and take ownership of their work. This trust allows individuals to develop their leadership skills and grow professionally.

Great leaders also support and advocate for their team members. They provide guidance, coaching, and resources to help individuals succeed. They celebrate achievements, recognise contributions, and provide constructive feedback for improvement. This support builds trust by showing that leaders care about the growth and development of their team members.

In a culture of trust, leaders encourage risk-taking and innovation. They understand that mistakes and failures are opportunities for learning and growth. Leaders create a safe space for team members to take risks and learn.

The best companies in the world are intentional about leadership development.

Effective leadership development programs are essential for success. These companies understand that leadership development goes beyond individual growth. It plays a vital role in the overall success and sustainability of the organisation.

Development programs within these top-performing companies often involve the CEO or leadership team. Senior leaders show the importance of strong leadership through their engagement and commitment.

Leadership development programs are essential because only leaders can produce leaders. Managers or Human Resources (HR) programs alone cannot develop individuals into effective leaders. Leaders play a crucial role in inspiring, mentoring, and supporting the growth of other leaders. Successful leaders attribute their success to guidance from other leaders. Learning from experienced leaders is invaluable and can shape an individual's leadership capabilities.

Companies that prioritise leadership development often see remarkable results. As mentioned with PepsiCo, they have become known as a "CEO factory," with a significant number of their alumni becoming CEOs of Fortune 500 companies. This success can be attributed to the company's rigorous and effective leadership development programs. Companies like PepsiCo use comprehensive leadership programs to create skilled leaders who drive success.

My Story

I understand what it feels like to be identified as a potential leader and groomed accordingly. Early in my career, the CEO at the time saw me as one of the company's key future leaders. He was intentional about giving me opportunities and experiences to propel me to the pinnacle of the organisation.

The first and most significant thing he did for me was to affirm my leadership abilities. I recall the day my CEO told me I would be the future president of the company, the second-in-command. It was a mind-blowing moment for me.

My CEO was deliberate in his approach to developing me as a leader. He gave me senior roles and expanded my job responsibilities. He supported my pursuit of further education by covering the costs. His actions exemplified what every leader should do in elevating and nurturing other leaders. His investment in my development enabled me to take on executive and leadership positions elsewhere.

Your experience underscores the transformative power of effective leadership development. By nurturing and empowering aspiring leaders, organisations not only cultivate a robust talent pipeline, but also foster a culture of growth, innovation, and long-term success.

ACTION PLAN

Whether you are in a leadership position or not, take a few minutes to do the following.

1. Write two or three names of people in your team, at work, or in your personal life you can mentor and develop in some way.
2. Write three actions you will intentionally take with those individuals to develop them.
3. For each one, write one action a week for twelve weeks you will do to meet those things identified in (2). For example, you can decide to send them an article to read a week or decide to meet with them for 30 minutes to mentor them.

_____
_____
_____
_____
_____
_____
_____
_____
_____
_____
_____
_____

If you are struggling to find someone you know, consider registering with a volunteer organisation seeking mentors. There are several organisations looking for people to mentor other people. This is a great way to develop and sharpen your coaching or mentoring skills.

Reflection and Looking Forward

In this chapter, we learned about the criticality of leaders developing other leaders and how the best leaders do this. Leaders focusing their time and effort on developing other leaders will lead to meaningful results, continuity, and the best decision-making. The best leaders and companies are intentional about developing leaders within their organisations. They recruit well, empower potential leaders, and create an environment for them to flourish and contribute.

One of the key aspects of great leaders is character. Poor leaders lack character. The next chapter defines character and the importance of it in leadership. Character is the foundation of trust in leadership. Without character, a leader can't inspire people.

Chapter 4 explores the profound importance of character in effective leadership. We explore why character is important, and its impact on decisions, relationships, trust, ethics, influence, resilience, and legacy. Examining character-driven leadership like Nelson Mandela shows that education does not guarantee success. It is character that safeguards success, achievement, and vision.

Read on as we uncover the indispensable power of character and discover how it shapes the very essence of leadership.

CHAPTER 3

CHARACTER IS KEY TO LEADERSHIP

Don't expect your success to carry you in life. Rather, let your success be carried by your character.
~ Myles Munroe

In the realm of leadership, success hinges on character and competence.

While both character and competence are important, it is character that often distinguishes exceptional leaders from the rest. Leaders often fail because of character flaws, but rarely because of incompetence. Character failures are more apparent and impactful, while incompetence can hide beneath the surface.

Knowing the importance of character is crucial, as you may become a top leader in the future. Character, defined as a commitment to unwavering values and standards, serves as the bedrock of leadership.

Character is not a gift given at birth, but something developed. It is not dependent on external circumstances, but revealed by one's actions when no one is watching.

The strength of a leader's character can be measured by the temptations they resist and the integrity they display. Integrity ensures consistency and alignment between words and deeds, building trust and credibility.

Steve Easterbrook's Story

The case of Steve Easterbrook, the former McDonald's CEO, is indeed a sad example of the importance or lack of character in leadership. His poor judgement and misconduct had serious consequences, despite his significant accomplishments.

Steve Easterbrook's success at McDonald's was impressive. He expanded McDonald's globally, remodelled the stores, and improved the drive-thru experience. These achievements led to the company's stock price doubling. However, his personal conduct and failure to uphold the company's values undermined his success.

Easterbrook's 2019 dismissal over a consensual relationship with an employee raised doubts about his judgement and following of company policies. He admitted failing to uphold McDonald's values, but the additional allegations of sexual misconduct and attempts to conceal evidence were more damaging.

Easterbrook's behaviour was inappropriate and not in line with McDonald's family-friendly image. As the CEO, he should have been acutely aware of the importance of avoiding such relationships with employees and setting a proper example. His actions violated the trust of the company's stakeholders.

The board of directors' investigation confirmed the allegations, exposing Easterbrook's dishonesty and fraud. This brought to the fore the severity of the situation. He had to pay back a large sum, including cash and stocks, because of his actions.

This case serves as a reminder that character is critical in leadership, regardless of the achievements and successes one may have. Leaders must uphold the values and ethical standards of their organisation. When leaders show poor judgement and engage in misconduct, it can harm the organisation's reputation and the trust placed in its leadership.

Steve Easterbrook's lack of character and poor decision-making led to his downfall. This example illustrates the impact of personal actions, both on the individual and the organisation.

Nelson Mandela's Story

The story of Nelson Mandela is a powerful example of moral character in leadership. Mandela's life and leadership are marked by resilience, forgiveness, and a commitment to justice and equality.

Nelson Mandela was a South African anti-apartheid revolutionary and politician who served as the president of South

Africa from 1994 to 1999. He devoted his life to combating the oppressive system of apartheid.

Mandela's character was shaped by his experiences and the challenges he faced. He spent 27 years in prison for his activism and resistance against apartheid. During his prison stay, Mandela remained strong and true to his beliefs. He educated himself, reflected, and envisioned a democratic and equal South Africa during his imprisonment.

One of the most remarkable aspects of Mandela's character was his capacity for forgiveness. Mandela advocated for reconciliation instead of revenge, despite the suffering he experienced. Upon his release from prison, he worked toward a peaceful transition to democracy and sought to unite a divided nation. Mandela recognised the need for forgiveness, understanding, and dialogue to heal South Africa.

Mandela's character also exemplified his commitment to justice and equality. He worked to dismantle apartheid. He believed in every individual's inherent worth and dignity, regardless of race or background. Mandela's leadership was guided by the principles of inclusivity, fairness, and respect for human rights.

Throughout his presidency, Mandela showed humility and a willingness to listen to others. He sought to bring people together, bridging the gaps that had long divided South Africa. Mandela's character as a leader was characterised by empathy, compassion, and a genuine concern for the well-being of all citizens.

Nelson Mandela's story is a testament to the transformative power of character in leadership. His commitment to justice, forgiveness, and equality shaped his life and inspired millions. Mandela's integrity enabled him to overcome obstacles and lead South Africa to democracy.

His legacy reminds us that leadership is not only for personal gain, but also for uplifting others. He taught us valuable lessons on integrity, forgiveness, and justice.

**ized *The Premise*

There are two primary reasons leaders fail to meet the expectations of their followers or employees: character and competence.

Failure in either aspect can lead to repercussions such as dismissal, or in extreme cases, legal consequences.

Character is often the major factor contributing to the failure of most leaders. Leaders often fail because of character flaws, while incompetence is less frequent. Incompetence can be more subjective, and those with true incompetence will theoretically have been weeded out before ascending to a leadership position. Character flaws are usually more obvious and have a greater impact.

Acknowledging character's significance is necessary for future advancement. It's thus essential to understand character and its importance in leadership.

What is character?

Character is a commitment to a set of uncompromising values and standards. It is intertwined with a person's values and represents their moral and ethical qualities. Upholding values is essential, and one shows true character by doing so. Character is the steadfastness and predictability of an individual; their values remain unchanged regardless of circumstances.

Character serves as the foundation of leadership. It encompasses traits such as honesty, integrity, empathy, humility, courage, and accountability. Leaders with strong character are trustworthy, inspiring others to follow their example. They prioritise ethical standards and moral principles. Leaders with excellent character are respected and admired, creating a positive work environment.

Character is self-imposed discipline, requiring personal accountability. It is not externally driven but revealed by one's actions when no one is watching. A leader's character is tested when overcoming temptations. Integrity is essential. It ensures consistency and alignment between words and actions.

Character is not an inherent gift or talent, but something that is developed. Leadership is not solely based on position or title, but on one's life and the reflection of their character.

Why is character critical to leadership?

Leadership is affected by character. Trust and credibility are built upon a leader's character. It shows integrity, honesty, and ethical behaviour. Leaders influence followers by inspiring and motivating them to be like them. A leader's character provides guidance and boosts confidence during tough times.

Trust and Credibility

Character is the foundation of trust and credibility. Leaders with strong character are trustworthy, dependable, and authentic. Leaders who demonstrate honesty and ethics earn respect. Trust is necessary for effective leadership as it builds open communication, cooperation, and followership.

Ethical Decision-Making

Character influences a leader's decision-making process. Leaders prioritise moral principles over personal gain. Ethical decision-making strengthens the leader's reputation and the organisation's ethical climate. By demonstrating ethical behaviour, leaders set an example for their team members and encourage them to act with integrity as well.

Influence and Inspiration

Leaders with strong character have a powerful influence on their followers. They model empathy, humility, and respect, which encourages others. Leaders who care, respect, and lead by example have motivated and committed followers. Character-driven leaders create a positive work environment that fosters loyalty, engagement, and high performance.

Resilience and Adversity

Leadership often involves navigating challenges and setbacks. In such situations, a leader's character plays a vital role in their ability to persevere and lead effectively. Leaders with strong character show resilience, courage, and determination in the face of adversity. They remain steadfast in their values, maintain a positive outlook, and inspire their team to overcome obstacles. A leader's character can provide stability and guidance during difficult times, instilling confidence in their followers and motivating them to keep moving forward.

Legacy

Leaders come and go, but the impact of their character lasts beyond their tenure. Leaders who prioritise character and ethical behaviour leave a legacy. They create a culture of integrity and values that outlive their time in leadership. Character-driven leaders have a positive influence on future leaders.

Nelson Mandela is perhaps one of the best examples of individuals who possess great character. He vocalised his anti-apartheid values, lived by them, and paid a significant price for holding those values. He endured over 20 years of solitary confinement. Despite being offered opportunities to renounce his stance on apartheid while in prison, he never gave in. He remained committed to his values without compromise.

Character safeguards a leader's success, achievements, and vision. Education alone cannot protect leaders from failure if their character is lacking. It is the alignment between words and actions that truly matters. People value character more than education.

Character is critical to leadership, as it forms the foundation upon which effective leadership is built. Leaders with strong character build trust, encourage ethical behaviour, and maintain a positive environment. Leadership experiences refine character and emphasise the need for ongoing growth.

ACTION PLAN

Character is the foundation for great leadership.
1. Write your values.
2. Write the values of a great leader you know personally.
3. Compare your values against the values of a leader you admire.
4. Write three things you can learn from your admired leader.
5. Ask yourself if there are any new values you may need to embrace to be the type of leader your team and colleagues can trust.

_____
_____
_____
_____
_____
_____

_____

_____

_____

_____

_____

_____

_____

_____

Reflection and Looking Forward

In this chapter, we learned what character is and the importance of character in leadership. We saw how a lack of character could destroy leaders and impact an organisation. We also saw how leaders with great character can transform communities and bring change to the world. We learned that character is a commitment to a set of values and standards without wavering.

In the book's first part, we talked about some key aspects of leadership. The next part will define what true leadership is. There are countless definitions and perspectives on the meaning of leadership. I will share a definition that encompasses several critical areas of leadership. Furthermore I will share some of key beliefs I have learned about what leadership is and is not.

PART TWO

Understanding Leadership: Principles, Qualities, and Practices

CHAPTER 4

DEFINING LEADERSHIP: PERSPECTIVES AND INSIGHTS

Leadership is influence.
- John C. Maxwell

Well-Known Definitions

In defining leadership, there is a plethora of definitions. A search on Google for the definition of leadership yields a long list of articles. According to Warren Bennis, various academic studies have generated over 850 definitions of leadership. This abundance of definitions highlights the absence of a consensus on how to define this concept called leadership.

Jacob Morgan asked 140 CEOs their views on leadership for his book *The Future Leader*. Each CEO provided different answers, demonstrating the lack of a common definition even among leading CEOs of our time.

Why is leadership difficult to define?

Why so many definitions? One simple reason is leadership depends on the context in which it is applied. Leadership can be defined differently in various areas of life, such as work, school, sports, or politics. The context and the specific situation determine how leadership is perceived or defined.

For example, the type of leader needed during a crisis differs from that required when everything is stable. Common themes emerge in most definitions despite contextual and situational variations. We take the definition for granted, so people don't think deeply about it.

People recognise good leadership when they see it, as it is felt and experienced. Likewise, they can identify poor leadership based on their own encounters. Leadership is not limited to one type of leader; it encompasses various personalities and backgrounds. For instance, Microsoft's former and current CEOs, Steve Ballmer and Satya Nadella, are distinctly different in their leadership styles, yet both are successful.

To illustrate the diverse definitions of leadership, I have listed ten definitions from respected leadership authors and CEOs of some of the world's largest companies.

1. *"Leadership is influence, nothing more, nothing less."*
   – John Maxwell, leading author on leadership
2. *"Leadership is translating vision into reality."*
   – Warren Bennis, leading author on leadership
3. *"Leadership is the capacity to influence others by unleashing the potential and power of people and*

organisations for the greater good." – Ken Blanchard, leading author on leadership

4. *"Leadership is having a compelling vision, a comprehensive plan, relentless implementation, and talented people working together."* – Alan Mullay, former CEO of Ford Motor Company
5. *"Leadership is helping people succeed, inspiring and uniting people behind a common purpose, and then being accountable."* – Paul Polman, former CEO, Unilever
6. *"Leadership is not a rank or a position to be attained. Leadership is a service to be given."* – Simon Sinek, leading author on leadership
7. *"Leadership is communicating to people their worth and potential so clearly that they come to see it in themselves."* – Stephen R. Covey, leading author on leadership
8. *"Leadership is the ability to step outside of your own point of view and see the bigger picture, with the goal of inspiring and guiding others towards a shared purpose."* – Bill George, former CEO of Mechatronics and leading author on leadership
9. *"A leader...is like a shepherd. He stays behind the flock, letting the most nimble go out ahead, whereupon the others follow, not realising that all along they are being directed from behind."* – Nelson Mandela, former president of South Africa

10. *"The definition of leadership is to influence, inspire, and help others become their best selves, building their skills and achieving goals along the way."* – Tony Robbins, leading motivational speaker and author

These ten definitions share common threads, including influence, goals, vision, purpose, people, relationships, service, accountability, perspective, and guidance.

No single definition is right or wrong. Leadership encompasses all these aspects. My 20+ years of studying leadership have taught me that personal leadership is essential. It is a prerequisite for and more important than corporate leadership.

This is one subtle difference that I see little in leadership from the many definitions. The focus is primarily on other people and achieving goals. While this is correct, it does not fully capture the true essence of what I believe leadership is.

Leadership is personal and a process.

Myles Munroe's definition of leadership is the most comprehensive definition I have come across. What sets it apart from others is its ability to guide individuals on the path to becoming a leader. It highlights that leadership is about self-discovery rather than assisting others. So, what is Munroe's definition of leadership?

Leadership is the capacity to influence others through inspiration, generated by a passion, motivated by a vision, birthed from a conviction, produced by a purpose.
  - Myles Munroe

This definition resonates with me because it encompasses various aspects of personal leadership. I believe this distinguishes exceptional leaders from the rest. Exceptional leaders possess clarity regarding their personal leadership. This quality distinguishes outstanding corporate or national leaders.

Munroe's definition outlines a clear process to follow, ultimately leading to influencing others. Influence is indeed the goal in leadership; not manipulation, but genuine influence. I will delve further into the distinction between the two later in this chapter.

The Premise

Within Munroe's definition, six key aspects are essential for leadership.

- Influence
- Inspiration
- Passion
- Vision
- Conviction
- Purpose

To understand this definition, reverse the order: Purpose to Influence. Progress through each step starting with Purpose. As you navigate through these steps, you transform into a person of influence, at which point, people refer to you as a leader. I will define each term in leadership and explain how they are interconnected.

The definition applies to personal leadership rather than in the corporate context. The principles outlined in this definition can also be applied in a corporate context.

Purpose

As mentioned, to grasp this unique definition, one must begin with purpose. But what is purpose, and what does it have to do with leadership?

Purpose, in this context, refers to your *why*. It is the reason for your existence on this planet. Many people find themselves at a loss when asked about their purpose. They either don't know or have never pondered it. Some dismiss it as flaky and irrelevant. I understand.

Initially, I, too, was sceptical about the concept of purpose. I failed to see its relevance to my everyday life, let alone its connection to leadership. Now, however, I realise discovering and understanding one's purpose is the most vital aspect of self-discovery.

I believe everyone has a purpose. Just because you may be unaware of your purpose doesn't mean you don't have one. Later in this book, I will detail how you can uncover your purpose. Ultimately, the goal of purpose is to delve within yourself and determine why you exist on this Earth. Another way to approach it is by asking yourself, "What problem am I here to solve?

CHAPTER 4

Simon Sinek's *Start with Why* applies to our individual lives as well as organisations. Sinek states:

All organisations start with WHY, but only the great ones keep their WHY clear year after year.

*

Regardless of WHAT we do in our lives, our WHY—our driving purpose, cause or belief—never changes.
~ Simon Sinek

Sinek emphasises that all great organisations begin with their WHY, not their WHAT. Starting with the WHY provides a reason or intention for the existence or creation of something. As described in Sinek's book *Start with Why*, individuals or companies that share core beliefs and values attract others. He uses the example of Apple as a much more successful company compared to others.

Apple doesn't advertise the fact that they sell computers or iPads; instead, they emphasise its tagline, "Think Different." People buy Apple devices to be different and challenge the status quo. The same applies to great leadership.

To be a great leader, it is crucial to understand and share your WHY. This is what forms the foundation of leadership, not an MBA or a leadership degree. Just like a house needs a solid foundation, leadership requires one too.

Ann Perry's Story

Ann Perry still holds the title of the longest-serving lollipop lady in the United Kingdom. Lollipop ladies help children cross the road safely to get to school. Come rain, cold, or heat,

Ann stands outside in the morning and afternoon to ensure children's safety.

Ann Perry bid farewell to her iconic role after an extraordinary 52 years of service. Back in 1969, the remarkable 80-year-old from Kingsbury, Tamworth, began her journey as a lollipop lady, filling in for someone for a mere six weeks. She did not know her temporary role would turn into a long-term commitment to keeping children safe.

Starting her day at 8:15 a.m., Ann patrolled the school crossing, ensuring the safety of children on their way to Kingsbury School. With the day's end, she resumed her duties in the afternoon, accompanying the students back home. She travelled 3,700 miles, staying dedicated to keeping children safe.

Reflecting on her noteworthy career, Perry remarked, "It was the best job in the world. I've loved every minute." Ann leaves behind a legacy of unwavering commitment and a profound impact on the community she served. Her decades of dedication as a lollipop lady will be remembered, cherished, and missed by all those whose lives she touched.

It's because of the WHY.

Although some may see Ann's job as monotonous, most people don't see it that way. In fact, the lollipop ladies have one of the most respected professions in England, with great admiration from the public. Many have been dedicated to this job for decades, serving with immense energy and passion. The late Queen Elizabeth II even honoured some for their service to local communities.

CHAPTER 4

Why do people hold them in such high regard? It's because of their WHY. Individuals like Ann could do other jobs, but they are passionate about the safety of children. Ensuring the well-being of children is a cause close to their hearts. It's a job one can only commit to if they are passionate about it.

Purpose gives life meaning.

Those who have discovered and embraced their purpose live focused and intentional lives. There are several high-profile individuals whose purpose is evident in their life's work, even if we don't know them personally. For instance, Mother Teresa's purpose was to help the poor. She dedicated her life to addressing poverty and found immense success and joy in that purpose. Nelson Mandela's purpose was to strive for equality for Black South Africans. Apart from these famous figures, there may be people around you whose purpose you can guess.

My purpose is to help others maximise their potential. This is the one thing that moves me to tears of joy. My family is always amazed when we watch movies about people fulfilling their potential and I become emotional during certain scenes. It is painful to witness individuals with great potential remaining stuck and not realising their full capabilities. That's all I see in people—their potential, not their current state. I envision what they can become.

Conviction

A strong sense of purpose often leads to deep conviction. Conviction can be defined as a held belief or opinion. It holds immense power. In a court of law, when someone is convicted of a crime, the judge has a firm belief or compelling evidence of their guilt. This conviction drives the judge to deliver a verdict. For a judge to impose a long prison sentence or the death penalty, the conviction of guilt must be firm.

Conviction plays a crucial role in advancing and holding onto our purpose. We may know our purpose, but without conviction, we may struggle to achieve or realise it. Conviction propels us forward, compelling us to take the next step. It explains why we may know something but cannot act.

Take, for example, the concept of healthy eating. Many people understand the benefits and purpose of consuming nutritious whole foods. They know that such a diet helps maintain weight and promotes better health. However, without strong conviction, this knowledge often fails to translate into action.

It is conviction that empowers individuals to make the right choices when faced with the option between healthy and unhealthy foods. It drives them to scrutinise food labels and conduct deeper research on the substances they put into their bodies. Vegans and vegetarians exemplify strong conviction about their dietary choices. They believe that meat or certain types of food are detrimental to human well-being.

Sometimes, conviction arises from personal crises. For instance, my wife developed severe intolerance to dairy and meat products. As a result, her belief that these foods are unsuitable for her health has become resolute.

We are prepared to defend and uphold our beliefs when we possess conviction. It becomes challenging to persuade someone to change their conviction. Just try convincing my wife to consume dairy—good luck with that! No matter how appealing the food may be, conviction runs deep within us, making it difficult to sway our held beliefs.

Without a doubt, your belief in your life's purpose will be tested. This is a positive thing. It is life's way of determining the strength of your conviction in what you claim to know and believe. Such tests often arise as opposition or challenges.

Greta Thunberg's Story

Consider the well-known environmental activist Greta Thunberg, one of the youngest activists of our time. With a strong conviction that humanity is destroying the planet, she has made a significant impact and continues to do so. Throughout her journey, she has undoubtedly faced opposition and criticism. Some would question her or her parents' decision to allow such a young person to miss conventional schooling. Critics may have scrutinised her exposure to the media spotlight. Yet, despite these opposing forces, she has persevered.

When she started, she had few supporters, and many would have doubted her potential for success. This is a common path; initially, few believe in you, and you may feel isolated. In fact, most of the time, people reject you or your ideas. It is conviction that allows you to see through this challenging phase of your journey. If you constantly seek acceptance from everyone, you will struggle to make progress.

When we possess strong convictions, we often have evidence or reasons supporting our beliefs. Sometimes, our evidence may not be rational to others, but it resonates deeply within us. In other cases, our beliefs make perfect sense, but others may not share the same conviction.

Once we discover our purpose, we must develop conviction to take the steps we need to take. This conviction may evolve or be ignited by specific contexts or personal experiences. Some individuals become convicted when they endure pain or hardship related to their purpose.

Leadership requires conviction

The primary reason conviction is required is for ourselves, not just to persuade others. Without conviction, as a leader, we lose influence, appearing indecisive and unreliable. We know people who say things without believing them. In contrast, we also know individuals who believe in their words. Even if we sometimes disagree or dislike their views, we respect them for their conviction.

Vision

Once you have discovered your purpose and conviction, you get a picture of where you are going. As Munroe puts it, vision is purpose in Technicolor. A vision is a vivid picture of your preferred future. Your vision is not related to your current situation. It is about where you see yourself in the future.

CHAPTER 4

Dr Martin Luther King Jr.'s Story

For example, Dr Martin Luther King Jr.'s purpose was to fight the oppression of Black people. He believed that oppression was wrong and fought for this. Dr King's vision encompassed a fully integrated society devoid of segregation or discrimination.

His vision was very clear. He described it in his 'I Have a Dream' speech.

> *"I have a dream that one day, little black boys and girls will be holding hands with little white boys and girls."*

To become a leader, you need a clear vision for your life.

You must be able to articulate your vision so others can visualise it. With a clear vision, you have a picture of what the destination looks like.

A personal vision is crucial, as it provides a sense of priority and focus. Once you discover your vision, it becomes almost inevitable that your key life decisions align with it. Vision dictates everything you do—the company you keep, the books you read, the places you go, and the opportunities you pursue. Vision has a profound impact on your life. It instils discipline. If you want a disciplined life, discover your purpose and vision. Vision makes things real to you, even if they may seem unrealistic to others.

It's essential to differentiate between vision and ambition. The two can be confusing. One simple way to distinguish them is that vision focuses on improving the lives of others, while ambition revolves around oneself.

Personal ambition and vision are different. As an example, consider my son's ambition to become a professional football player. From a young age, he dedicated his childhood to playing football. Currently enrolled in a top-level football academy in England, his life revolves around the sport. However, this ambition primarily benefits him. Most times, personal ambition may align with one's vision. In my son's case, his ambition in football may ultimately lead him to get closer to his vision.

A true vision never leaves you. It occupies your thoughts, permeates your dreams, and is always on your mind. Witnessing others pursuing something similar can evoke powerful emotions within you. Your vision will persistently haunt you because it is the source of your fulfilment.

Many people feel dissatisfied with their jobs because they sense they're in the wrong place, without being able to explain why. They constantly change jobs in search of satisfaction. Often, they have not taken the time to understand and embrace their purpose and vision.

As mentioned before, purpose is inherent within us. On the one hand, we are aware of it, but we have been educated to not believe in our inner selves. We have been trained to compare ourselves to external standards or other people.

Passion

The next stage in the leadership process is passion. Passion is a strong desire or drive. When someone has a passion for something, it means they have a deep desire to pursue that thing. So how is passion generated? It is caused when you have a clear and compelling vision of a preferred future that resonates with you profoundly.

Passion is who you are, not what you do. It is an internal energy that fuels your pursuits. As Ken Coleman, author of *How to Find Your Passion* explains, you can identify your passion by looking at two key elements: emotion and devotion. If something triggers positive emotions within you and you will devote significant time and effort to it, it shows your passion. Having a clear vision of a preferred future stirs a desire within you to act. This desire to act is your passion. Passionate individuals are often committed to their pursuits.

The term *passion* is often misused or confused with mere interest. While interests are things you enjoy doing, passion goes beyond that. The Latin origin of the word *passion* is *pati*, which means to suffer. Passion, in its truest sense, implies being willing to endure and suffer for the sake of a cause. This drives people to take actions that may seem baffling to others.

Passionate individuals will make sacrifices and endure hardships for their cause. They choose to pursue certain endeavours irrespective of monetary rewards. For example, Nelson Mandela's fight against apartheid was not merely an interest, but a rooted desire to see change. He would suffer for the cause, and he did.

When you discover your passion, you attract people and gain attention. You are driven and dedicated to your pursuits.

My Wife's Story

My wife has a passion for seeing children being healed from emotional hurt. Her vision is to see children who have gone through difficult and traumatic experiences become free and live a life of fulfilment. She left well-paying traditional jobs to start her parent-coaching business to impact families and children.

It has not been a straightforward process. First, she has given up the security of getting an income regularly. She was very good at her job and in secure employment, having taught in some of the leading secondary schools in England. She also had to undergo some training to get some requisite qualifications.

Starting a service business is no mean feat. The first few months of her business were tough, with very few customers and lots of spending on Google ads and marketing. She overcame challenges and her business is flourishing with satisfied customers.

Passion sets people apart from those who lack it in a particular area. In most aspects of life, it is those who possess the desire to persevere through tough and challenging times who ultimately succeed. You will face challenges, it's only a matter of when.

Passion empowers you to overcome challenges. The desire must be greater than the obstacles or difficulties you encounter.

CHAPTER 4

We cannot fake passion; it is an emotion that stems from within. It is rooted in a deep sense of conviction and having a clear vision of your preferred future.

Inspiration

The next stage in the leadership process after passion is inspiration. Do you feel inspired by my wife's passion and vision? I certainly do. I am amazed by her passion and dedication to children.

My wife is one of the smartest people I have ever met, and she could have done anything she wanted and been financially rewarded. However, she dedicated herself to a cause that people may have seen as risky and challenging. She doesn't have to say much to motivate me to support her. I'd do the same for a stranger. I am eager to assist her on her journey and willing to sacrifice my time and resources for her.

The Story of the 2022 Women's Euro Football Final

Have you ever wondered why we pay to watch top performers in sports, music, or any field? It's because of the passion and discipline these athletes exhibit which leads to excellence.

I remember the 2022 Women's Euro football final, which England won. It was a significant victory for the country, as it marked their first international football trophy, men's or women's, in over 50 years. This event captured the attention of many people, even those who don't regularly watch football, or women's football.

People were awed by the team's performance throughout the tournament, culminating in their triumph over Germany in the final.

Following the tournament, it was reported that many girls took up the sport of football. It also inspired the England Men's team to perform well in the subsequent World Cup tournament. The ripple effects of inspiration are far-reaching.

Passion Sparks Action

When you witness individuals who are passionate and dedicated to a cause, it ignites a desire within you to act, contribute, and participate. This voluntary action is where the magic happens. How do you get people to change direction or behaviour willingly without resorting to manipulation or coercion? The answer is inspiration.

Inspiration encourages people to think differently and step out of their comfort zone. Inspiration can spread from one person to another. Inspiring leaders can cultivate a shared vision, purpose, and potential.

A lack of inspiration is one reason top performers leave companies. When there's a lack of vision or a vision cannot inspire, passion within the company dwindles and people lose their motivation. They show up at work for a paycheck.

While this may be satisfactory for some individuals, top performers are typically not driven by money alone. They crave inspiration; if they don't find it, they disengage and move on. When you lose your top performers, your business declines or underperforms.

CHAPTER 4

Influence

Influence is indeed the crux of leadership. According to the dictionary, influence is the ability to affect or change how someone or something develops, behaves, or thinks. We all have a measure of influence in our lives, and the level of influence we possess is a good indicator of our leadership.

Munroe's definition of leadership resonates because it emphasises that influence is about who we are, not just what we do. Discovering and being convicted of purpose leads to influence. It is a process of self-discovery rather than techniques or manipulation.

It is important to note that influence can be positive or negative. Dictators like Hitler were influential, but their impact was abhorrent. The crucial factor lies in whether we inspire or manipulate people. True influence inspires action, while manipulation through fear or deceit forces change against will. We achieve true influence when people decide to follow us, trust us, and believe in the destination and the journey we are taking them on.

Many individuals find themselves in jobs with leaders they don't trust or want to follow. It could be fear of unemployment or the need to maintain a certain income. I have been in that position myself. I'm sure most of us have experienced similar situations. The outcome is often a lack of motivation, then resentment, and finally departure from the organisation.

TRUE LEADERSHIP

My Story

Just as the pandemic was nearing its end in 2022, my family and I left the church we had been attending for two years. We felt unsettled for various reasons and wanted to try a different local church for a few weeks.

We found a new church in a nearby city and started attending. On a Sunday, I chatted with a man named Ben while waiting to get my kids from the Children's Centre at the new church. We exchanged pleasantries and introduced ourselves. I was impressed by Ben's warmth and genuine interest in me. I had noticed him during church services giving announcements and assisting in various capacities.

It wasn't until subsequent weeks that I discovered Ben was the lead pastor—the "Big Boss" of the organisation. I was astonished. What blew me away wasn't his title, but that he never came across as the Big Boss. Ben was humble, and genuinely cared about people. That was my enduring impression.

Throughout those four or five weeks, he never sought the spotlight; instead, he put his team first and worked in the background. I was inspired, and from that day onward, I attended this church and followed this kind of leader. Ben's leadership influenced our Sunday church selection, despite other options.

Today, I contribute my time and money to support the church—all of it inspired by Ben.

I share this story to illustrate how leaders can inspire people to change and act in a certain way. Ben was not manipulative; he embodied the values and treatment he wished for people when they entered his church.

CHAPTER 4

Leadership involves positively influencing others and inspiring them to change. It is about serving others and putting their needs above our own. True leaders understand the power of influence and use it to make a positive difference in the lives of those they lead.

ACTION PLAN

1. Think about your own understanding of leadership based on your experiences and beliefs. What does leadership mean to you? Write your personal definition of leadership, considering the aspects and themes that resonate with you the most.
2. Explore the concept of purpose: Reflect on the importance of purpose in leadership as discussed in the chapter. Consider your own purpose in life and how it relates to your leadership potential. Take time to delve within yourself and uncover your *why* or the problem you are here to solve. Write your thoughts and reflections on your purpose.
3. Examine the role of conviction: Consider the role of conviction in leadership and how it can drive you to pursue your purpose. Reflect on your own convictions and beliefs. Write examples of situations where your convictions have influenced your actions or decisions. Consider any challenges or opposition you have faced and how your convictions helped you stay committed.

Reflection and Looking Forward

In this chapter, you learned about what leadership is and the process of becoming a true leader. I emphasised that true leadership has more to do with who you are than what you do. Leadership is about influence. Becoming a true leader is a journey that begins with purpose and culminates in influence.

CHAPTER 4

In the next chapter, I want to share key principles that have affected my leadership journey the most. You will discover five principles that will transform your understanding of leadership. You will uncover the secrets of becoming a true leader and learn how to inspire others, make impactful choices, and embrace your purpose.

Leadership is not about titles or positions—it's about influence and the willingness to serve others. Join me on a transformative journey of self-discovery and unlock your true leadership potential. Step into a world where leadership is accessible to all, and experience the power of becoming a leader who inspires and empowers others. Are you ready to embark on this extraordinary adventure?

The path to transformational leadership continues in Chapter 5.

CHAPTER 5

FIVE KEY PRINCIPLES I HAVE LEARNED ABOUT LEADERSHIP

Leadership is not about titles, positions, or flowcharts. It is about one life influencing another.
~ John C. Maxwell

Over the past 20 years, I have dedicated myself to studying the subject of leadership. What has been even more valuable are the opportunities I've had to assume leadership roles at various levels in a wide range of organisations. These experiences have provided me with invaluable lessons.

I have often taken the time to reflect on the topic itself, as well as on my own abilities as a leader. I have experienced both success and failure in my leadership journey. These experiences have helped me internalise some key leadership principles. These principles and beliefs shape how I collaborate with others, make decisions, and present myself.

In this chapter, I share these key principles and hope they benefit your leadership journey.

Principle 1: Everyone has the capacity to lead.

"Everyone has the capacity to lead, but you must become a leader" (Myles Munroe).

My Story

During my childhood, I developed a fascination with plants. My parents would buy me seeds to plant in our garden and entrusted me with the responsibility of caring for those plants. I remember receiving tomato seeds and feeling a strong desire to grow tomatoes in our garden, which we could later use for cooking and eating. I took the seeds, prepared the soil, and performed the steps.

After watering the area diligently for a few days, the plants germinated. However, I neglected the basic care they needed. I stopped watering the plants, and the area where they grew was not suitable, with poor soil quality, among other issues. Predictably, I never saw my tomatoes. It was a sad outcome, but not surprising.

Although the small seeds in my hand had the potential to become tomatoes, they needed to undergo a process to fulfil that potential. In my case, that process never took place. Why? Because I did not follow the steps to nurture their growth. I failed to water them, provided poor soil conditions, and deprived them of essential nutrients.

CHAPTER 5

Leadership is not restricted to a particular group of people based on race, class, education, or age. I believe everyone has the capacity to become a leader. However, possessing the capacity is not enough; one must embark on the journey of becoming a leader by following a specific process. Leadership is about influence, so if you can influence others, you can lead them.

As mentioned in my earlier definition of leadership, it is a process that begins with purpose and culminates in becoming a person of influence. Like a seed, you need the right environment to grow and become influential. Leadership is not a gift or an automatic trait, but develops.

My conviction is such that I view everyone I encounter as a potential leader. Viewing people this way changes how I interact with and engage them. It shapes my feedback and advice, allowing me to recognise their strengths and potential.

I am also mindful that having the capacity to become something is not sufficient on its own. Just as possessing talent is not enough to win medals, recognising leadership potential is not the sole requirement. We must acknowledge everyone's capacity to be a great leader.

Unfortunately, many people are unaware of their own leadership potential. They do not see themselves as leaders, and believe leadership is reserved for a select few, chosen by others. This misconception needs to be debunked. I am passionate about helping others discover their leadership potential. It is essential to understand that leadership will look different for each person. Leadership is not contingent on having a formal title. In fact, if you rely on your title to lead, you are not a true leader.

Principle 2: Leadership is a Choice

"Leadership is not a position or title; it is a choice"
(Steven Covey).

Leadership is based on choices and actions, not hierarchy or title. It suggests that anyone can choose to be a leader. Your official role or authority does not matter. All you need to do is embody certain qualities and leadership behaviours.

Leadership is about influencing and inspiring others to work together. It goes beyond the boundaries of a job title or a position within an organisation. Formal leadership roles come with certain responsibilities and decision-making authority. However, they do not make someone a leader people want to follow. True leadership is not dictated by a job description or an organisational chart; it is a choice to step up, take the initiative, and positively impact others.

Anyone can exhibit leadership skills beyond formal settings or organisational structures. It extends to various aspects of life, including personal relationships, community involvement, and societal change. Leadership can be demonstrated by community action, advocacy for a cause, and inspiring others.

Mother Teresa's Story

Despite lacking a formal title or high-ranking position, Mother Teresa was one of the most influential figures in the world. She had audiences with presidents, princesses, and dignitaries, and received many accolades, including the Nobel Peace Prize. Countless books and studies have been dedicated to her, offering valuable leadership lessons. She was a true leader with a clear purpose and unwavering passion, making her influential. Her decision to leave Ireland and serve the poor in a poverty-stricken part of India was a conscious choice.

This principle holds great importance to me because people often confuse leadership with titles. I understand why this confusion arises, but having a title does not make you a leader whom others want to follow.

As you become influential, people may bestow titles upon you in many aspects of life. I have nothing against titles; they can be wonderful and hold significance. However, you should never lead based on your title or rely on it to guide others. Relying on your title and authority won't help you go far or bring out the best in people. People are *inspired* to act, not dictated or coerced in a particular direction. Are people following your instructions out of respect and trust, or just because you pay them?

Personally, I have embarked on an intriguing journey in my career, holding both prestigious and less prestigious titles. Recently, I transitioned from senior manager to sales representative, focusing on individual contribution. My decision surprised many people. They couldn't comprehend why I would leave a higher-profile role for a lower-profile one. Even my mentor, whom I respect, cautioned me about the differences I would encounter in my less prominent position. He was right to remind me. He wanted to ensure that I was making the right choice.

When I changed roles, titles played no part in my considerations. I made the change because it aligned with my long-term career plan and promised greater benefits in the future. I was not willing to jeopardise my long-term growth for the sake of a title.

Please don't misunderstand me; I appreciated my previous title. It made me feel important, opened doors, and garnered closer attention from others. However, in the grand scheme of things, it has not defined me. I am still the same person, and I continue to exert influence in my current position. In fact, it has compelled me to sharpen my influencing skills. While you may occasionally rely on your title to accomplish certain tasks, it should never be your primary strategy.

Regardless of your position or title, you can still become a leader. A title is not a prerequisite for leadership. This challenges the traditional notion that leadership is given to you as a title. Leadership is about influence. You are a leader if you can influence others to take action. You have the choice to influence others, regardless of your formal position.

Principle 3: Leadership is more about self-discovery.

"True leadership is not about having followers or subordinates; it is about embracing self-discovery and understanding who you are" (John C. Maxwell).

CHAPTER 5

The common thinking about leadership is you need people following you or working for you before you are a leader. That if you manage a team of people, then you are in leadership.

In the last twenty years of studying great leaders, and my personal experience, I have concluded that leadership is more about discovering who you are. The definition I gave about leadership in the previous chapter validates this. To be a leader, you first need to discover your purpose. When you discover yourself and choose to pursue that path, you will influence people, and they will call you a leader.

Great leaders, like Dr Martin Luther King Jr., Mother Teresa, and Gandhi, share a common trait, even without titles. They had a purpose and a conviction that took over their lives.

Dr Martin Luther King Jr.'s Story

Dr Martin Luther King Jr. devoted his life to pursuing racial equality and justice in America as a charismatic leader and prominent figure in the civil rights movement. He wanted more than just ending segregation and civil rights for African Americans. King strived to create a unified society without racial divisions through his speeches, nonviolent protests, and dedication to justice.

As Dr King delved deeper into his activism, he discovered a profound truth about his own identity and purpose. He recognised that his role extended far beyond being a spokesperson for the oppressed. King realised he had a unique ability to galvanise and unite people under a common cause. His encounters with discrimination and injustice enabled him to sympathise with others' struggles. Irrespective of race, this revelation propelled him to become a champion for all marginalised communities.

King's vision was not limited to achieving legal equality; he aimed to address the underlying attitudes and beliefs that perpetuate racism. He understood that true transformation requires a fundamental shift in society's mindset. By promoting nonviolence, love, and understanding, King challenged not only the laws, but also the hearts and minds of the American people. His goal was to build a society that celebrates diversity, embraces equality, and values the inherent worth of every individual.

Dr Martin Luther King Jr.'s journey as a civil rights leader was a profound exploration of self-discovery and purpose. He recognised that his mission extended far beyond the fight against segregation; it encompassed the creation of a society that acknowledged and addressed racial issues at their core. King's vision sought to transform hearts and systems, and his dedication motivated many to fight for equality. His legacy reminds us to find our true selves and purpose.

The best leaders are more interested in discovering who they are and living it out than in proving themselves to others. When you spend more time expressing who you are, you become free from other people's opinions. Insecure leaders seek external validation and may prioritise pleasing others or proving their worth to maintain their position. This is why insecure leaders are sometimes attached to titles. Amid proving yourself or worrying about other people, you lose yourself.

You can no longer be who you really are. You lose your essence and influence when you are not being your true self.

Principle 4: Followers are Attracted to True Leaders

"Leaders do not seek followers; followers are attracted by true leaders" (Lao Tzu).

My Story

One of my career's most memorable moments occurred while flying to a business meeting. To provide some context, I held a significant position as a senior executive in the company. Given my influential role, I was approached by a junior colleague who was also on that flight. I recognised her, as she was managing a project I was involved in. I invited her to sit next to me since there was an available seat.

She started the conversation by saying, "Gabriel, I want to be like you," and I listened attentively. "How can I achieve that? I want to work under your guidance." Her words took me by surprise, and I was unsure of how to respond. It was a heartwarming moment that moved me.

I expressed my gratitude for her kind words and told her how much they meant to me. Before answering her question, I wanted to understand what qualities she admired in me. Therefore, I asked what specifically drew her to aspire to be like me. She explained she appreciated my approachability and genuine care for others, which set me apart from other executives. Considering there were six levels of hierarchy separating us, her admiration was both unexpected and touching.

Having grasped her perspective, I offered her guidance on how to cultivate similar qualities within herself. I encouraged her to discover her purpose and stay true to herself. While she desired to work under my leadership, it was at this point that I realised true leaders do not need to actively seek followers. By embodying authenticity and pursuing personal growth, people gravitate toward genuine leadership. Since then, colleagues at different levels have expressed their willingness to work with me and follow my lead.

Discovering your purpose and embracing your leadership potential attracts others to you. Rather than actively seeking followers, being passionate about what you do and inspiring others is crucial. True leaders are not preoccupied with pursuing or persuading people to follow them. Instead, their unwavering passion and compelling vision make others want to collaborate and contribute.

In many hierarchical organisations, there is an assumption people will willingly follow those in positions of authority. While formal power may yield compliance, it falls short of true leadership. People will do the minimum required, and if they dislike their leader, they may even undermine their plans. True leaders focus on developing themselves to inspire others. This natural magnetism encourages people to align themselves with such leaders.

CHAPTER 5

Mother Teresa's Story

Mother Teresa never aimed to lead, yet she became a leader when followers joined her mission to aid the poor. This stands in contrast with many leaders today, where the pursuit of leadership itself often takes precedence. Her clear and compelling vision to eradicate poverty from the world made her a leader, inadvertently rather than intentionally.

While she never sought to become a leader, she emerged as one because of her remarkable mission and the profound impact she made on society. Mother Teresa's followers were motivated by her genuine compassion, empathy, and selflessness, not by personal gain or pursuit of power.

One of the primary reasons people regarded Mother Teresa as a true leader was her clear and compelling vision to eradicate poverty from the world. She possessed a belief that everyone, regardless of their social or economic status, deserves love, care, and basic human dignity. This vision resonated with individuals who shared her concerns about the plight of the poor and marginalised. Mother Teresa's ability to articulate and live her vision inspired many to join her cause.

Mother Teresa's leadership was characterised by her persuasive nature of actions. She led by example, demonstrating an unparalleled level of humility and self-sacrifice. Her willingness to tend to the sick, comfort the dying, and provide care to those in dire need showcased her profound dedication and commitment. She immersed herself in the lives of the poor to connect with them on a deep emotional level, demonstrating that true leadership is about service and prioritising others' needs.

Mother Teresa's leadership style also stood in stark contrast to the prevalent leadership paradigms of today's society. Unlike those who seek leadership roles for personal gain, recognition, or influence, Mother Teresa's focus was solely on her mission. She never used her position to exploit others or further her own agenda. She invested all her energy into helping the destitute and neglected. This authenticity and lack of self-interest made her an exemplary leader in the eyes of those who followed her. Her legacy reminds us that true leadership is about positively impacting others, not titles or positions.

Principle 5: Leadership is Service

"Leadership is not about being in charge.
It is about taking care of those in your charge" (Simon Sinek).

Servant leadership is one of the most important principles I have learned about leadership. It entails recognising that the highest form of leadership is serving others.

Servant leadership is a profound and transformative principle that lies in serving others first. It goes beyond traditional leadership models that prioritise power, authority, and control. Instead, servant leadership is centred around the idea of leaders being attentive, empathetic, and focused on meeting the needs of their followers.

Servant leadership recognises that leaders prioritise the growth and well-being of those they lead, rather than personal gain or recognition. Servant leaders put their followers first rather than their own authority and goals.

It is a philosophy that acknowledges the interdependence of leaders and their followers. It recognises that leadership is manifested through acts of selflessness, humility, and a genuine desire to uplift others.

Queen Elizabeth's Story

Even the revered late Queen Elizabeth of Great Britain understood this concept. In her 70th Jubilee message, she expressed her commitment to continue serving with all her heart. The Queen, one of the most influential people on the planet, comprehended that her role was about serving her country and the world. This highlights one paradox of leadership: being the head while also being a servant.

Service in leadership involves prioritising the needs of others above your own. Simon Sinek's *Leaders Eat Last* emphasises that true leadership costs prioritising others' needs over one's own.

While the principle of servant leadership is well known, it is not commonly practised. People often agree with it in theory but struggle to implement it in practice. The challenge lies in understanding what it means. Serving others instead of oneself goes against corporate leadership norms. People aren't bad, they just don't prioritise the needs of others.

Servant leadership is not a concept that can be learned and implemented overnight. It goes beyond intellectual understanding; it is deeply rooted in one's belief system and how they view life. Changing one's belief system takes time and genuine transformation.

In senior corporate positions, self-prioritisation, office politics, and power-seeking are common. This often leads to manipulation, backstabbing, and focusing on self-serving needs. This is not true leadership.

I have witnessed both exemplary servant leaders and oppressive leaders. A servant leader is easily recognisable when you see or work with one. They exhibit humility and a genuine interest in others.

Here are ten characteristics I have observed that differentiate traditional leaders from servant leaders. It is important to note that there is a spectrum.

Traditional Leaders	**Servant Leaders**
Lead using power and control	Lead by example
Motivate using manipulation/techniques	Motivate by inspiration
Focus on position/title	Focus on serving
Focus on personal ambition	Focus on others
Base success solely on results	Base success on growing others and results
Do more speaking than listening	Do more listening than speaking
Take credit for success	Share credit for success
Pass responsibility of failure	Take responsibility for failure
Manage people	Empower people
Produce followers	Produce leaders

⟨Extreme ──────────────────────── Extreme⟩

CHAPTER 5

Servant leadership is not a new concept, but leaders rarely discuss and embody it. Ken Frazier and Frank Blake embody the servant leadership principles discussed in this book. Interestingly, both individuals came from non-traditional backgrounds and became CEOs of Fortune 500 companies. They were both lawyers, and never envisioned themselves as CEOs when they joined their respective companies. They both assumed their CEO positions during times of crisis. Ken and Frank are powerful advocates of servant leadership. They openly talk about it as their leadership style.

From a practical perspective, one common approach they use to implement servant leadership is the concept of the inverted pyramid. This method is employed to embed a servant leadership culture within an organisation. See the illustration below. The traditional leadership model places the CEO at the top of the hierarchy, with employees and customers at the bottom. However, in the servant leadership model, the structure is reversed. The CEO is at the bottom, while the customers and employees are at the top.

With the inverted pyramid, the burden rests with the CEO. For example, communication between the CEO and employees changes. Rather than pushing vision and mission statements down into the organisation and hoping it trickles down, CEOs must push their communication up the organisation. This is a much more challenging task. It means that CEOs must ensure that the vision, mission, or any relevant communication are compelling and inspiring enough for the layers in between to capture and take ownership of the communication and then communicate it upwards.

Another example is receiving customer feedback. In a traditional leadership model, customer feedback rarely reaches the top unfiltered, if it even makes its way up the chain. Customer feedback flows down the organisation in the inverted pyramid model. It's the CEO's responsibility to get customer feedback with no filters.

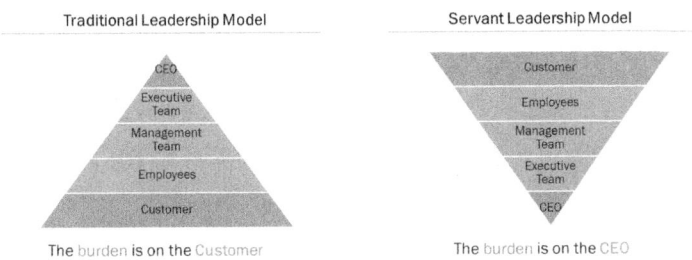

The inverted pyramid represents a true cultural shift. It communicates the CEO position in the hierarchy to customers and employees. Top-of-the-pyramid frontline employees are motivated to serve customers and make the right decisions.

I have worked in organisations where even middle management is hesitant to make simple decisions because no one wants to take ownership. There is a culture of escalating everything up the chain. Decisions are pushed up the organisation in an inverted pyramid structure, allowing for faster decisions from employees.

Servant leaders lead differently from traditional leaders. Chick-fil-A, Southwest Airlines, Nordstrom, and UPS are all advocates of servant leadership.

CHAPTER 5

ACTION PLAN

1. Write the names of a traditional leader and a servant leader (not mentioned in this book). Identify three characteristics of each that differ from the other.
2. Assess yourself as a leader or someone who leads you. Pick three characteristics of a servant leader from the list of ten in this chapter and grade yourself or your leader 1 to 10.

Reflection and Looking Forward

In this chapter, I talked about some of the leadership principles that have impacted my life and leadership journey the most. These principles and beliefs reflect my leadership style today or whatever advice I give others. In the next chapter, I discuss the type of leaders people want to follow.

CHAPTER 6

THE TYPE OF LEADER PEOPLE WANT TO FOLLOW: TRAITS AND QUALITIES

Become the kind of leader that people would follow voluntarily, even if you had no title or position.
~ Brian Tracy

Alexander the Great's Story

There once existed a remarkable leader named Alexander. Born with a silver tongue and a heart full of empathy, he possessed a unique ability to connect with people and create a profound impact on their lives.

Alexander's unwavering care for people was legendary. He treated everyone with respect, no matter their rank. He would often visit the homes of the less fortunate, sitting by them and listening to their concerns. Alexander had an innate ability to understand the struggles of others and empathise with their hardships. His genuine concern for their well-being touched the hearts of all who crossed his path.

But Alexander's caring nature extended far beyond mere words. He was a leader who believed in the transformative power of action. When disaster struck, he led the relief efforts, tirelessly working alongside his followers to provide aid and support. He established welfare programs, built hospitals, and implemented educational initiatives to uplift the lives of the marginalised. Alexander's dedication to improving the lives of his people was not driven by political gain or personal ambition; it came from a deep-rooted desire to see everyone thrive and flourish.

Through his consistent acts of kindness and selflessness, Alexander became the embodiment of hope for the oppressed. The mere mention of his name brought solace to the downtrodden and inspired them to dream of a better tomorrow. People knew they could rely on him, not only for his words of encouragement, but for tangible help when they needed it the most.

Trust was the cornerstone of Alexander's leadership. He understood that without the unwavering trust of his followers, his vision for a better society would remain unattainable. Alexander acted with utmost integrity, making decisions that were guided by a deep sense of morality and fairness. He held himself accountable to the same standards he expected of others and never wavered in his commitment to transparency and honesty. This unwavering trust allowed his people to stand united, confident in their leader's genuine intentions and steadfast dedication to their well-being.

Alexander's impact extended far and wide, transcending the boundaries of his kingdom. People from distant lands marvelled at his ability to lead with compassion, give a helping hand, and earn the trust of his followers. Leaders across the world sought to emulate his leadership style, recognising the profound impact he had on his people's lives.

Even in the depths of history, Alexander's legacy endures. His name is whispered with reverence and admiration, a testament to a leader who cared deeply, helped selflessly, and earned the unwavering trust of his people. His story serves as a reminder that true leadership is not measured by conquests or accolades, but by the genuine care, assistance, and trust a leader brings to the lives of those they serve.

The Premise

People respond to leaders who care about them, can help them, and can be trusted.

Answering the question of what kind of leader people want to follow can be tricky, as there are multiple perspectives to consider. Most studies and reports on leadership focus on the leader's perspective, usually focused on the leader's traits, qualities or skills.

It might be more valuable to approach this question from the perspective of the followers or people being led. What do they want from their leaders? How would they want to feel during a one-on-one interaction?

John Maxwell offers an insightful perspective on this matter. He suggests that every follower ask three fundamental questions about their leaders:

1. Do you care about me?
2. Can you help me?
3. Can I trust you?

If we examine these questions, we can see they revolve around the follower's needs. People are primarily interested in themselves. They are less concerned about the leader's intelligence, strategic abilities, or title. Instead, their underlying concern is whether the leader adds value to their lives.

Do you care about me?

According to John Maxwell, this question reflects the need for compassion. People are not concerned about how much knowledge their leader possesses; they want to know how much the leader genuinely cares about them.

Shockingly, McKinsey research indicates that 34% of individuals leave their jobs because of an uncaring leader. This statistic shows how important leadership behaviour is to employee retention and job satisfaction. Leaders' lack of concern for employees' well-being can create disconnect, dissatisfaction, and disengagement. Many job departures are influenced by problems with managers or company leadership, as per our experiences and our colleagues.

Whether expressed explicitly or not, people ask this question. In every one-on-one meeting with team members or when addressing employees, individuals seek reassurance regarding their leaders' interest in their lives. They desire someone who will listen to their pain, deepest thoughts, and concerns. Displaying empathy and taking an interest in their personal lives and passions is crucial.

To show that you care about your team members or colleagues, it is important to:

Listen actively: Provide a safe and open space for individuals to express their thoughts, ideas, and concerns. Actively listen to their words, paying attention to both verbal and non-verbal cues.

Show empathy: Put yourself in their shoes and try to understand their perspective. Validate their emotions and show understanding and compassion.

Build personal connections: Take an interest in their lives beyond work-related matters. Get to know their hobbies, interests, and aspirations. Celebrate their successes and milestones.

Provide support: Be there for your team members when they face challenges or struggles. Offer guidance, resources, and assistance when needed. Let them know you have their back.

Be authentic: Lead with honesty, integrity, and transparency. Authenticity builds trust and fosters a sense of genuine care.

Remember, caring about your team members goes beyond asking how they are doing. It requires active engagement, sincere interest, and a willingness to support their growth and well-being. You create a positive environment that promotes loyalty and job satisfaction. It sets the foundation for an effective leader-follower relationship.

Can you help me?

This question reflects the need for competence. Every employee wants to know if their managers or leaders possess the ability to help them. This help could include career growth, promotion opportunities, fulfilling aspirations, and finding enjoyment in work. Most individuals want to progress in their careers. As we have all experienced, we often rely on our managers or bosses for guidance and support in advancing our careers.

Feeling that your manager is unable or unwilling to provide the help can be disheartening. Have you ever believed you deserved a promotion or were ready for more significant responsibilities? Yet despite multiple attempts, you could not get help from your manager to gain the promotion. Many people who face this scenario ultimately choose to leave their current role or even the organisation.

A manager's lack of support can cause frustration and demotivation. Employees want leaders who have the competence and influence to facilitate their progress. They seek managers who can provide guidance, mentorship, and opportunities for development. When leaders take a keen interest in their team member's career, it creates a sense of trust, respect, and mutual investment.

To show your competence and ability to help your team members, consider the following actions.

Understand individual aspirations: Take the time to understand your team members' career goals, ambitions, and areas of interest. Tailor your support and guidance based on their unique needs and aspirations.

Provide developmental opportunities: Identify and provide growth opportunities, whether through additional responsibilities, special projects, or training programs. Help individuals gain the skills and knowledge they need to progress in their careers.

Offer mentorship and coaching: Act as a mentor or coach to your team members, providing guidance and support as they navigate challenges and pursue their goals. Share your expertise, insights, and lessons learned from your own experiences.

Advocate for your team: Recognise and promote the accomplishments and potential of your team members. Act as a champion for their advancement and advocate on their behalf when appropriate.

Create a culture of learning and growth: Foster an environment that encourages continuous learning, skill development, and innovation. Support initiatives that enable team members to broaden their knowledge and expand their capabilities.

By demonstrating competence and helping team members, you create a supportive environment that empowers individuals to make progress. This fosters employee engagement, satisfaction, and loyalty.

Understanding the importance of the "Can you help me?" question and taking steps to support your team members' growth can significantly impact their careers and overall job satisfaction. It strengthens the leader-follower relationship and contributes to a positive and thriving work environment.

Can I trust you?

This question delves into the character aspect of leadership. Trust serves as the foundation for effective leadership. People want to know if they can trust their managers or leaders. They seek reassurance that your words, actions, and lifestyle align and are consistent. They want to be led by someone trustworthy, who will lead them to success with integrity.

At my previous job, a leader preached values but acted contradictorily. Despite their charisma and convincing speeches, I lost trust in this leader. I couldn't rely on their words or actions, and it impacted my motivation to give my best. Unfortunately, this lack of trust permeated the company culture, affecting our results. Customers sensed our lack of trust in our leaders, so they took their business elsewhere.

Trust becomes even more critical at the manager level. Employees want to believe in their direct managers. They need to know that if they confide in their managers, their concerns will be confidential and addressed. They don't want their managers to use information against them or pay lip service to their worries.

I have made the mistake of giving mere lip service to a concern raised by one of my direct reports. I remember a contractor on my team who was worried about losing her job during contractor terminations. She confided in me, and

I empathised with her situation, promising to do everything possible to help her remain in the company. However, I failed to take meaningful action or fight for her case. She eventually lost her role, and I could sense the disappointment and loss of trust in our final interaction. I had let her down, breaking her trust in me.

Building trust as a leader involves several crucial aspects. One way is by demonstrating responsibility. Are you the type of person who takes ownership of initiatives, stepping up when others hesitate? Do you proactively do what is right?

Another way to cultivate trust is by giving credit to others for successes while taking responsibility for failures. I learned this from a remarkable leader I encountered. He always credited his team's accomplishments but took full ownership of mistakes. This approach had a profound impact, sending a clear message he had his team's back and building a strong foundation of trust.

Showing trustworthiness requires consistency between words and actions, taking responsibility, and showing integrity. Trust is earned through sustained actions over time. Trust is essential for effective leadership.

ACTION PLAN

Conveying Those Qualities as a Leader
1. Write the names of two leaders you know and respect and two you know but don't respect.
2. For each of those four leaders, ask yourself the three key questions followers ask: 1) Do you care about

TRUE LEADERSHIP

me? 2) Can you help me? 3) Can I trust you? — and rate answers to each question from 1 to 10 (1 lowest rating and 10 highest).

3. Add up the scores for each leader and then compare the gap between leaders you respect and leaders you don't respect.

This exercise shows you the stark contrast between the type of leader you want to follow and the type of leader you don't want to follow.

CHAPTER 6

Reflection and Looking Forward

In this chapter, I have attempted to define in simple terms the type of leader people want to follow. I have examined it from the perspective of followers who ask three important questions: Do you care about me? Can you help me? and Can I trust you? Many of the qualities required to answer these questions are more closely related to who the leader is, rather than what they do. Followers are interested in who their leader is and why they do what they do. People follow your *why* rather than your *what*.

So, how can you become the type of leader people want to follow? How do you define your *why* and create the influence that attracts people to you?

The last part of the book explores how to become a leader people want to follow, the rewards and challenges of leadership, and the power of gratitude.

PART THREE

Becoming That Leader and Valuing It Once You Are

CHAPTER 7

THREE STEPS TO BECOMING A LEADER PEOPLE WANT TO FOLLOW

A true leader has the confidence to stand alone, the courage to make tough decisions, and the compassion to listen to the needs of others. They do not set out to be a leader but become one by the equality of their actions and the integrity of their intent.
— Douglas MacArthur

Early in my career, I landed my dream job. It was a senior leadership role. However, I had this question – how do I become the type of leader people want to follow?

I had no leadership experience. My experience in the industry was non-existent. I felt insecure. The only thing I had was a lot of knowledge about leadership. I had studied leadership by reading books, had great mentors, and a passion for learning. I was fortunate my father had modelled what true leadership was. However, it is one thing to have the knowledge and another to live it.

I pondered for several weeks how to lead in my new role. I decided to focus on two things: being authentic, and applying leadership lessons. One approach I consciously avoided was pretending to be someone else. It was tempting frequently to act in a certain way to prove my leadership or justify my role, as I had seen others do.

Over the years of doing this dream job, I gained self-confidence and continued refining my leadership style. I made mistakes and received critical feedback from people I respected. This journey gave me a strong conviction about what I am about to share with you. Being a leader people want to follow is more about who you are than what you do.

While I was young and inexperienced, people, including seasoned executives, followed my lead. They were willing to listen and agree with my direction. Some even took a risk and changed jobs to join me on a mission. So, how did I become the person and leader I am today?

The Premise

I can break it down into three steps:

Step 1 - Discover yourself and your gifts.

Step 2 - Refine and serve your gifts.

Step 3 - Love people.

CHAPTER 7

The power of your leadership lies in leading from your place of value. Your value is your diamond.

STEP 1: Discover yourself and your gifts.

My Story

My journey to self-discovery started when I was sixteen, just a few weeks before my final secondary school exams and prom. It took a painful moment to set me on this path.

As the exams and prom approached, I needed a date for prom night. This was a big deal. A good friend of mine introduced me to a friend of his girlfriend. I went to her house one weekend, sort of like a date. While with her and her friends, I realised I preferred watching a football game on TV over showing genuine interest in her. I was socially awkward back then, so it wasn't surprising.

What unfolded in the following days changed my life. The incident spread throughout the entire school, and I became the target of mockery, portrayed as a socially awkward person. Many of my male friends laughed and ridiculed me, and no one wanted to hang out with me. Being a 16-year-old under peer pressure, I felt lonely and depressed. It was the first time in my life that I felt alone. I didn't know what to do. At that moment, my only option was to pray to God.

I was anxious about my upcoming exams, the most significant after six years of schooling. I had worked hard, but I knew that my emotional state could jeopardise all my efforts. So, I prayed to God, asking for help with my exams.

The good news is that I performed well in my exams. Surprisingly, I achieved the second-best results in my school year. I was awarded a plaque I still cherish today. This unexpected outcome gave me a tremendous boost, unlike anything I had experienced before.

This whole drama may seem trivial, but not for me. This moment ignited a burning desire within me to discover who I truly was. I wanted to break free from the opinions of others. I had an innate longing to uncover and embrace my authentic self. It has been a journey of over twenty-five years, and I am still on that journey.

Who are you?

Do you know who you truly are? Have you ever asked yourself this profound question? Significant moments in life prompt us to delve deep within. Some may have yet to embark on this introspective journey. Personally, I am grateful to have explored this question early in my life.

Today, we are bombarded with influences that can overshadow our sense of self, causing us to lose sight of our uniqueness. We often conform to societal expectations, as if pressured to fit into predefined moulds. Our parents, with the best intentions, may have specific ideals and desires for who they want us to be. They may unintentionally deny their children the chance to understand themselves.

CHAPTER 7

It is crucial to acknowledge that the answer to the question of who you are can only come from within. Yes, you hold the key to unlocking your true identity. No one else can define you with absolute certainty. Don't let other people define you; the truth is within you. It is a personal journey of self-discovery that only you can undertake.

Why is it so important to know who you are?

Let's explore several compelling reasons why it's so important to know who you are.

1. **True Potential**: Understanding your true identity allows you to tap into your full potential. Recognising your strengths can help you discover hidden talents. Embracing your authentic self opens a world of possibilities.
2. **Self-Worth:** Knowing who you are gives you a sense of security that external validation or the approval of others cannot provide. Knowing your values, beliefs, and boundaries makes you less influenced by others' opinions. Your sense of self-worth and inner stability are not easily shaken.
3. **Authenticity:** Embracing your true identity leads to true fulfilment. You create a sense of harmony and purpose by aligning your actions, choices, and relationships with your core values. Authenticity brings contentment beyond possessions or achievements.

4. **Empower others**: Understanding who you are allows you to positively impact others. When you are in touch with your true self, you radiate authenticity and inspire those around you. By embracing your unique qualities and sharing your gifts with the world, you can uplift and empower others to embrace their own identities.

5. **Authentic relationships:** Knowing yourself leads to authentic relationships. When you have a deep understanding of yourself, you can communicate your needs, values, and boundaries effectively. This clarity lets you build relationships that match your true identity, creating genuine connections and growth.

6. **Personal empowerment**: Understanding your identity empowers you to take charge of your life. You become the author of your own story, making conscious choices that align with your values and aspirations. Empowerment gives you confidence and strength to tackle difficulties and pursue your ambitions.

7. **Life purpose and direction**: Knowing who you are provides a compass for your life's purpose and direction. Understanding your passions, strengths, and values allows you to identify and pursue paths that align with your authentic self. This clarity guides you towards meaningful goals and a sense

of fulfilment as you contribute to something larger than yourself.

8. **Self-acceptance and compassion**: Embracing your true identity allows for self-acceptance and self-compassion. You acknowledge and embrace all aspects of yourself, including strengths, weaknesses, and imperfections. Self-compassion brings greater well-being and inner peace.

9. **Authentic expression**: When you know who you are, you feel confident and comfortable expressing your true self. You can share your unique perspective without fear. This self-expression allows you to shine your light and inspire others to do the same.

10. **Personal growth and self-discovery**: Understanding your true identity is an ongoing process of personal growth and self-discovery. As you continue to explore and learn more about yourself, you uncover new dimensions, expand your horizons, and develop as an individual. This continuous growth brings a sense of vitality and fulfilment to your life.

In summary, knowing who you are can have profound benefits that extend to various aspects of your life. From fostering authentic relationships to empowering personal growth, understanding your true identity enhances your well-being, purpose, and impact on the world. Embrace the journey of self-discovery and allow your authentic self to glow.

The journey of self-discovery is an ongoing and transformative process. Embrace your uniqueness and understand your true essence. Remember, the answer to the question of who you are lies within you, waiting to be discovered, embraced, and celebrated.

A Golden Buddha's Story

In 1957, the Thai government decided to construct a new port and highway, which required the land occupied by monks to be used. As a result, the monks had to move a shrine that housed a clay Buddha.

The government arranged for movers to handle the relocation of the Buddha. They employed a crane to move it, but cracks began appearing on the clay Buddha during the process, causing panic and concern about further damage. In response, they brought a larger crane in for the move, which was planned for the following day, taking weather into account.

However, a monk noticed something in a crack of the clay Buddha and used a torch to inspect it. To his surprise, he discovered a golden light emanating from within. He left to retrieve a chisel and excavated the clay surrounding the Buddha. As he continued, he revealed a magnificent golden object hidden beneath the clay. Excited by the discovery, he informed the other monks. That night, they used chisels to uncover the rest of the golden Buddha.

When the movers arrived the next day, they were astonished and bewildered to find a golden Buddha instead of the expected clay one. This extraordinary Buddha, which dates to the period between the 1230s and 1430s, had been covered in clay centuries ago to conceal its true value. Today, this golden Buddha is estimated to be worth over $250 million and holds the distinction of being the largest golden object in the world.

How do you discover yourself and your gifts?

Like the clay Buddha, our true value lies within us, not outside of us. To understand our real selves, we must cut through the noise, lies, misinformation, prejudices, and beliefs that surround us. Today, people often try to define us, telling us who we are and what we can or can't do. Labelling can come from parents, teachers, or others, and have a lasting impact on our lives.

Consequently, many struggle with self-esteem issues, which may manifest in various aspects of their lives. Often, these challenges can be traced back to their childhood. No one can determine or assign our value; we must discover it from within. The clay does not define our identity; breaking away from it is necessary to unleash our true selves. Shedding the clay of our identity may not be easy, but it helps us discover our inner gold.

Discovering ourselves sets us on a path to becoming the best versions of ourselves. What does this mean? It means fulfilling and maximising our true potential. But what is potential? It's what we are capable of but haven't yet achieved. We often underestimate our potential. Success should not be measured by comparing our accomplishments to those of others; instead, it should be measured against what we could have accomplished.

When we embrace our true selves, we attract people and position ourselves for unimaginable success. People notice something unique about us when we discover our authentic selves. This is why gold is valuable—it's rare. Clay is common, and therefore, free. The more unique and authentic we are, the more valuable we become. While blending in may provide a sense of security, standing out allows us to change the world and make a significant impact.

When we live unauthentically, we experience stress. Much of the stress people face today arises from doing things they dislike. UC Berkeley research studied the connection between daily activities and stress. The study showed that unpleasant tasks were linked to higher stress and lower well-being.

People take jobs to pay bills or because of societal expectations. You might think I live in a fantasy world where everyone can do what they want. But you'd be wrong. When we discover ourselves, we are more likely to choose jobs or start businesses that align with our desires. The target is to make every job as close to perfect as feasible. Throughout my career, I have always done what I wanted, understanding the end goals and achieving them in my own unique way.

There are many paths to success. We imitate others when we don't know our true selves. It's important to learn from others, but never to imitate them. I have learned a great deal from other leaders, yet I lead in my unique and authentic way.

We don't have to pretend or imitate when we are true to ourselves. A sense of security is something we all crave. Sometimes, we call it being comfortable in our own skin. The more we discover our true selves, the more comfortable we become with who we are.

True fulfilment in life comes from pursuing what matters to us, not what others expect of us. Thick layers of clay can hide the gold within us. There are many layers to unravel before we can understand our deepest desires.

To discover your true self, there are **three fundamental things** you want to understand – **your purpose, your vision, and your strengths.**

Understanding these will put you on a path to becoming the type of leader people want to follow.

Your Purpose and Vision

Purpose and vision go hand in hand. This is your *why*. I would say this is the starting point to discovering who you really are. Understanding your purpose will give you a foundation to begin to focus and live a life of fulfilment. So, what is purpose in one's life?

How do you find your purpose?

It may seem like a big question to answer, but it is easy to find. The reason is that purpose is inherent. It is within you. The purpose of anything is inherent in the thing. For example, if I gave you an iPhone for the first time, you would discover its purpose quickly. This is because the purpose of an iPhone is inherent in the iPhone. Experimenting with features and reading the manual helps understand the phone's purpose.

Your purpose is within you and should be easy to discover. The problem is that no one has ever shown or encouraged you to find it.

Vision is related to your purpose. As per the definition I mentioned in earlier chapters, vision comes from conviction, which comes from purpose. So, to know your vision, you must first understand your purpose.

I have learned different ways to find your purpose from various leaders, some of whom have helped me find mine. I'll share the ones that have resonated with me and I've seen work with many people.

The key to finding purpose is design, desire, and distinction. The design of a thing is always created with its purpose in mind. The purpose of an aircraft is to fly, so its body is designed to fly. So, study your design. In your case, your design will reflect your personality.

Purpose is also revealed by desire. What is your natural desire? You must distinguish between your interests and desires. Desire is like your passion.

Next, think about what distinguishes you from others. What do you do better than others effortlessly? You can refer to this as your talent or your gifts. A combination of all three things will help you reveal your purpose.

In thinking about your design, desire, and distinction, answer these eleven questions:

1. What problem in humanity are you longing to solve?
2. What makes you angry?

3. What would you like your legacy to be?
4. What makes you cry?
5. What would you rather be doing?
6. What would you do all day long if money was not an issue?
7. What do people compliment you most about?
8. What dreams do you have that never go away?
9. What is the unique contribution you want to make to the world?
10. What are you passionate about?
11. Reflect on the skills and abilities that come naturally to you. What are you good at?

Once you ponder these questions and answer them, you will get a sense of your purpose and see your vision. Your purpose will be something that primarily benefits others and not yourself, in the same way a tree bears fruit not for the tree to eat but for humanity to eat. I have learned this from studying great leaders who have discovered their purpose. It is never about them. It is about other people.

The paradox is that your purpose is the key to your ultimate fulfilment. Money, material things, titles, etc., will never give you true happiness and fulfilment. Fulfilling your purpose will.

To find your purpose and vision, you must give yourself permission to dream big and imagine the future you desire. Let go of any limiting beliefs or self-imposed boundaries. Envision the impact you want to create, the goals you want to achieve, and the life you want to lead. Allow yourself to think beyond your current circumstances and envision a compelling future.

Look for inspiration from others who have pursued their purpose and vision and made a significant impact. Read books, listen to podcasts, or attend seminars by thought leaders and visionaries in fields that resonate with your interests. Seek guidance from mentors or coaches who can provide insights and support as you explore and refine your purpose and vision.

Finding your purpose and vision is often a process that takes time. Be patient and open-minded and allow yourself to explore different paths and possibilities. Embrace failures and setbacks as learning opportunities and be willing to adapt and evolve as you gain more clarity. Remember, discovering your purpose and vision is a personal and individual journey.

It took me over five years to become very clear about my purpose and vision. I wrote it down, and every time I read it, I smile, and it still resonates even after 20 years.

"My purpose is to encourage people, so they can truly discover themselves and achieve and experience true success."

Every word in my purpose statement is meaningful to me. They are real. When I use the word encourage, it is not simply to say something nice to someone. It is a commitment to do whatever it takes to encourage someone. I am prepared to do anything that encourages someone to find themselves and achieve true success. I will make any personal sacrifices to help someone in this context.

True success here is not about money or titles. It is fulfilling and experiencing what we are born to do. Nothing makes me happier than seeing other people pursuing or living out what they care about. I cry whenever I watch a movie where the character achieves something deeply personal. I know it is not real, but I get so emotional, as that is what I want for people more than anything else.

Purpose does not mean you quit your job. What you want to do is live out your purpose in your job. In most cases, they are not mutually exclusive. In my case, I have always been able to shape my roles to allow me to live purposefully. When you live a life of purpose in your work, the work becomes much easier and more enjoyable. There will always be parts of your job that you hate, but it should not be most of your work. No question, the more you get clearer about your purpose, it may lead you to do something different. This is especially true if you have a clear vision of your purpose.

Once you discover your purpose and vision, you have discovered your value.

Your Strengths (or your gifts)

I am a big believer in the strengths movement. I believe this is where you find your unique value to the world. Combining your purpose, vision, and strengths gives you a unique place in the world.

Your strengths are what you excel at naturally.

Many of us are not aware of our unique strengths. We may have an idea, but we are not sure. Like the clay Buddha, we are covered in clay and, for some of us, trained to focus on our weaknesses.

Various studies have shown that individuals are happier and more fulfilled when they use their strengths at work. Companies are now fostering a strength-based culture.

How do you identify your strengths?

There are established personality tests that can help us identify our strengths and weaknesses. Tests such as Clifton's StrengthsFinder, Myers-Briggs, Enneagram, Working Genius, and DISC are examples I have used. I recommend you explore some of these tests and others to see which one interests you. They all focus on different aspects of personality.

Personally, I have completed all of them to better understand all aspects of myself. They are not all perfect, but they are fairly accurate. When I see the results, I am not surprised, and it just helps confirm what I have always thought. They are a tool to aid in finding better language for self-discovery. These tests are not there to *tell* you who you are but to *reveal* who you are. So, in all honesty, the result you get in most cases should resonate with you.

Once you have identified your strengths, the next step is to leverage them effectively. Knowing your strengths alone is not enough; you must apply them purposefully. Understand how your strengths can contribute to your overall goals, whether in your personal life or in a leadership role. Reflect on how you can use your strengths to make a positive impact on others and achieve greater success.

It's important to acknowledge that strengths can be developed and refined. Continuous learning can help us improve our known strengths and discover new ones. Seek opportunities to use your strengths. Embrace a growth mindset and be open to expanding your capabilities.

In the realm of leadership, understanding your strengths is essential for effective leadership. It allows you to play to your strengths, delegate tasks that align with others' strengths, and create a balanced and high-performing team. Recognise and use the strengths of your team to maximise collective potential.

Leaders who are aware of their strengths can also inspire and empower others. When people see their leaders using their strengths to achieve meaningful outcomes, it motivates them to do the same. Showing the importance of strengths-based leadership can help others find and use their strengths.

The strengths movement offers a powerful framework for personal and leadership development. Harnessing our unique strengths can lead to more fulfilment in life. Take the time to discover and embrace your strengths and leverage them to make a positive difference in your life and those around you.

STEP 2: Refine and serve your gifts.

Diamonds are highly coveted and valuable gemstones, often associated with wealth and luxury. But have you ever wondered why diamonds hold such immense value? The rarity of diamonds is a major factor contributing to their high worth. Diamonds are rare, unlike iron ore, which can be found in many locations.

To locate diamond deposits, companies invest billions of dollars and years of exploration, sometimes up to a decade.

Finding diamond mines is no small task. Specialised equipment is required to dig deep into the earth, and sometimes negotiations and payments must be made to landowners to secure mining rights.

The process of diamond extraction is just the beginning. During the extraction process, various stones are unearthed, including worthless ones and rough diamonds. While the worthless stones are discarded, the few precious, rough diamonds undergo meticulous procedures. Immersing the rough diamonds in a hot chemical bath can remove impurities and rocks. The result is a pure, yet still rough, diamond.

At this stage, the diamond is called a rough diamond. It must undergo cutting and polishing, known as refinement. A plan is developed to determine the ideal cut, size, angles, and other factors before cutting and polishing any rough diamond. The ultimate aim is to create a diamond that reflects and refracts light optimally, showcasing its brilliance and sparkle. Skilled diamond polishers, who are trained and knowledgeable, carry out this specialised process.

Like the journey of a diamond, once you have discovered your true value (i.e., strengths), it is crucial to refine it. Initially, your strengths may be raw, unpolished, and characterised by sharp edges. Even in this state, they hold incredible worth.

But just imagine the possibilities of a refined version of your strengths. To refine your strengths, you must develop the skills and knowledge. Common sense is a good starting point, but gaining knowledge and learning from others is vital.

CHAPTER 7

Refining your strengths is a process that takes time, but it should also be an enjoyable and fulfilling one.

Let's explore four ways to refine your strengths.

1. **Seek Knowledge and Continuous Learning**: Invest time and effort in acquiring knowledge and expanding your understanding of your strengths, especially as it relates to your purpose and vision. Read books, attend workshops, take courses, and stay updated with the latest trends and developments. The more knowledge you gather, the more refined and valuable your skills and insights become. This is why I am obsessed with leadership. Most of my strengths point to visionary leadership. So, most of my interests lie in this area. There is a popular saying that *Leaders are Readers*. I believe this is true. The best leaders understand the importance of continuous learning.

2. I am not a natural reader, but I read 20+ books yearly. How do I do this? I mostly read books that feed my purpose, vision, and strengths. Guess what? I love reading those books. I have a vast library of books. Occasionally, I read other types of books, but most align with my vision. Thankfully, today there is easy access to information. Books are cheap, and many free videos and podcasts are available.

3. **Find a Mentor:** Seek guidance and mentorship from someone accomplished in your field. A

mentor can provide valuable insights, advice, and support as you navigate your journey of growth and refinement. Learn from their experiences and tap into their wisdom to enhance your own capabilities. Mentors are very critical, as they have been through a similar journey you are embarking on. They can help speed up your growth if you find the right one.

4. **Cultivate a Growth Mindset**: Adopt a mindset that embraces growth and embraces challenges as opportunities for learning and improvement. Embrace failure as a steppingstone to success, and view setbacks as valuable lessons. A growth mindset enables you to continuously refine your abilities, adapt to new situations, and overcome obstacles with resilience. Just as seeds require time, nurturing, and the right conditions to grow into thriving plants, our potential also needs a similar approach. It is essential to recognise that the realisation of our full potential is not an overnight process. It requires patience, effort, and a commitment to continuous growth.

5. **Seek Feedback and Act Upon It**: Actively seek feedback from others, whether it's from colleagues, mentors, or clients. Listen to constructive criticism and use it to refine your skills and approaches. Incorporate feedback into your self-improvement efforts, adjusting and enhancing based on

the insights you receive. The areas I have grown the most have come from soliciting feedback. We often have blind spots, and no amount of reading will help. We need people around us with different perspectives to help us identify our blind spots. Sometimes, it may not be blind spots. It may be a strength we just have not identified or paid attention to, so it can be positive feedback.

By applying these strategies, you will refine your strengths, enhance your capabilities, and become a more influential and impactful individual in your chosen domain. You will live a purposeful life. Remember, refinement is an ongoing process, and the journey toward unlocking your full potential is continuous.

Jim Rohn was an American entrepreneur, author, and motivational speaker. He was regarded as one of the greatest personal development and motivational speakers of his time. Rohn advocated personal growth, goal setting, self-discipline, and continuous learning as the path to success.

Jim's works taught me a lot about becoming more valuable. His belief was that success was linked to how valuable you are in the marketplace. He believed personal development was the key to becoming more valuable. He said, "Work harder on yourself than you do on your job." The principle of becoming more valuable is in line with refining your strengths.

Three principles create the perception of increased value.

1. **Significance:** Strive to make a significant impact in a chosen domain. This should be related to your purpose and vision. Seek opportunities to contribute and create positive change. Identify areas where you can add value and make a difference. By aiming for significance, you position yourself as someone who stands out and creates a lasting impact.
2. **Uniqueness:** Embrace your individuality and nurture your unique strengths, skills, and perspectives. Find what makes you stand out and use it to provide something of worth. Emphasise your personal brand and showcase your unique value proposition. You become more sought after and valued for your distinct contributions when you emphasise your uniqueness.
3. **Originality:** Cultivate a mindset of creativity and innovation. Strive to bring fresh ideas, perspectives, and solutions to the table. Don't be afraid to think outside the box and challenge conventional thinking. Embrace your creativity and let it shine through your work. By offering originality, you become a source of inspiration and novelty, enhancing your value in the eyes of others.

Focus on significance, uniqueness, and originality to stand out. These qualities can open up new opportunities and recognition. Embrace these aspects as you refine your value and make a lasting impact in your chosen endeavours.

CHAPTER 7

Serve your gifts.

Once you discover your strengths, you must use them to benefit others. As you serve your strengths to others, a reciprocal dynamic emerges. When you serve others expecting nothing in return, people are more likely to reciprocate in various ways. This reciprocity may not always happen immediately, or in the way you expect, but in my experience, it exceeds expectations. The key is to approach service with a mindset of positively benefiting others rather than seeking personal gain.

To serve others effectively, it is crucial to be secure within yourself. This is where the importance of the first principle comes into play. People will sense your authenticity when you are secure in your own values and motives. They won't assume you have ulterior motives but will desire to help and support you.

Believing in your worth enables you to serve others faithfully and with integrity. It is through serving others that you attract people to your leadership. Remember, servant leadership is not about only serving when others are watching, but also when no one is watching. Embracing small opportunities to demonstrate your strengths exhibits leadership. Remember, your highest impact will always be in your strengths.

Leadership is about seizing opportunities. By embracing the service mindset, you position yourself to make a positive impact and inspire others. The more you serve, the more people recognise you as a leader, and the more opportunities to lead will come your way.

Service should be about helping others with humility and empathy. By embracing this approach, you not only contribute to the success of others, but also cultivate a reputation as a leader worth following.

Serving your value is a transformative mindset that can elevate your leadership to new heights. When you recognise and embrace your unique talents and strengths, you can serve others with authenticity, purpose, and impact.

STEP 3: Love people.

The third step in becoming the type of leader people want to follow is loving people.

When the word *love* is used in a business context, it often evokes a range of reactions. Some view it as a weak and irrelevant subject in business. It is not a word commonly used in discussions or practices related to business and leadership. In my experience, I have rarely seen organisations or HR departments prioritise love in a professional setting.

The discomfort or hesitation around discussing love in business is understandable. It can feel unconventional or even inappropriate to bring up such a personal and emotional concept in a professional environment. The reason behind this reluctance lies in a misunderstanding of what love means and how it is essential to effective leadership.

Emphasising love in leadership is not to promote warm feelings, but to use it as a powerful tool for business goals and building relationships. Leading with love creates a positive environment where individuals feel respected.

In this context, love has nothing to do with romantic or emotional love as we know it. Rather, it encompasses a broader understanding of love as a set of attitudes and behaviours that prioritise the well-being and growth of others. It involves showing care, empathy, and understanding towards employees, colleagues, and stakeholders. It means treating people with kindness, patience, and respect.

Leaders can foster a sense of belonging and trust among team members by leading with love. This leads to increased engagement, productivity, and loyalty. When people feel genuinely cared for and supported, they are more likely to go above and beyond to achieve organisational goals. Love in leadership is not a soft approach but a strategic choice that yields tangible results.

Leaders need to recognise that love and business can coexist. By incorporating love into their leadership style, they can positively impact both the bottom line and the well-being of their employees. It requires a shift in mindset and a willingness to challenge traditional notions of leadership, but the rewards are worth it.

What is love?

"Love" carries different meanings and connotations depending on the context. The English language lacks distinct words for different forms of love, making it difficult to express their nuances. The Greek language provides a more comprehensive framework for understanding different aspects of love.

Let's explore the five types of love to help us understand the specific type of love I am referring to for leaders.

1. **Eros**: This type of love refers to romantic love, often associated with desire, attraction, and physical intimacy. It is the love typically experienced between romantic partners.
2. **Philia**: Philia represents the concept of deep friendship, camaraderie, and affectionate love. It is the love shared between close friends, characterised by loyalty, trust, and mutual support.
3. **Storge**: Storge relates to familial love, particularly the natural affection and bond between parents and children, siblings, or other family members. It embodies a sense of familiarity, comfort, and unconditional care.
4. **Philautia**: Philautia encompasses self-love. It can be both healthy and unhealthy, depending on its manifestation. Positive self-love is accepting and taking care of oneself, while negative self-love is selfishness, narcissism, and arrogance.
5. **Agape**: Agape is regarded as the highest form of love. It is selfless, unconditional love that extends beyond personal relationships. It encompasses compassion, empathy, and care for others. Acts of kindness, forgiveness, and a genuine concern for the well-being of others characterise agape love. This is the type of love I recommend leaders embrace in their leadership.

Agape love has nothing to do with emotions; it is one of choice. We express it through our actions, attitudes, and care for others. Selflessness, generosity, and a desire for the well-being of others expecting nothing in return characterises it.

Here are some key points to emphasise.
1. **Agape love is a choice:** Agape love prioritise others' well-being rather than being driven by emotions or personal gain. It goes beyond fleeting feelings and is grounded in a genuine concern for their welfare.
2. **The impact of agape love is profound:** When we practice it, its effects can be transformative for both individuals and businesses. Showing patience, forgiveness, and understanding leads to better relationships and outcomes.
3. **Agape love is liberating and enriching:** Choosing to love selflessly frees us from the constraints of ego, selfishness, and narrow self-interest. It allows us to experience a sense of fulfilment and purpose as we derive joy from seeing others flourish and succeed.
4. **It reflects our humanity:** Agape love is considered a high form of love, highlighting our capacity for empathy, compassion, and care. We recognise everyone's worth and dignity through agape love.
5. **Agape love fosters personal growth and forgiveness:** It teaches us to love even those who don't deserve it. This transformative aspect of agape love enables personal growth, healing, and reconciliation.

Incorporating agape love into our interactions and leadership positively impacts individuals and business culture and success. It promotes a sense of belonging, cooperation, and shared purpose, allowing people to thrive and contribute their best.

So, how do you develop this love?

I am not sure if anyone can fully develop this type of love within themselves. I recognise we are all humans and have many imperfections. Nevertheless, I believe we should have this type of love as a personal goal and strive towards attaining it. To embody agape love, you must start with **self-discovery** and understanding your value, then **refining and serving** your value.

These two elements form the foundation for loving others. Loving someone expecting nothing in return may sound easy, but it is not in reality. Through my personal journey, I have reached a stage in my life where I can consciously decide to love someone expecting nothing in return. This transformation did not happen overnight; it was a gradual process that involved deepening my understanding of who I am and discovering my purpose. This journey of self-discovery has given me peace and security, allowing me to love without expectations. I believe you can also get there.

CHAPTER 7

Agape love unlocks your leadership gift and greatness.

Agape love unlocks your leadership gifts and enables you to reach your full leadership potential. Without love, you will not realise the full extent of your influence. It doesn't matter if you're intelligent, with degrees from prestigious institutions like MIT or Oxford. It doesn't matter if you hold an MBA or have achieved outstanding success in your career, even rising to the position of CEO. Even if you possess excellent communication skills and are a compelling speaker, these qualities alone will not maximise your leadership greatness. Why? Because true leadership is about serving others, and you cannot genuinely serve people you don't love.

Here are four key steps to love others.

1. **Love yourself**: Start by caring for yourself. Recognise you cannot give what you don't possess. This is an important principle. Take the time to understand and appreciate your own worth and value. When you have a deep sense of self-love, it will better equip you to extend love to others.

2. **Understand people's needs**: Take the initiative to understand the needs and aspirations of others. Go beyond surface-level interactions and seek to understand their dreams and goals. Focus not only on where they are but also on where they are headed. This empa-

thetic understanding will help you connect with them on a deeper level.

3. **Find ways to meet those needs**: Once you understand people's needs, seek ways to meet them, whether offering support, guidance, resources, or lending a listening ear. Find meaningful ways to contribute to their well-being and growth. Actively look for opportunities to make a positive difference in their lives. Make no mistake – meeting the needs of others may sometimes mean telling them the hard truth. It could mean helping them find a different job or making hard decisions. The key is doing it lovingly, in their best interest.

4. **Have no expectations of return**: Love expecting nothing in return. True love is selfless and unconditional. Avoid attaching expectations or seeking personal gain from your acts of love. Embrace the joy and fulfilment that comes from giving with no strings attached.

By following these four steps, you cultivate a mindset of love and contribute to the well-being and growth of others.

ACTION PLAN

1. Write your purpose statement. It does not have to be perfect, and it will evolve. Use the questions I suggested earlier in this chapter to help you identify your purpose.

2. Invest in completing at least two different personality tests. If you want recommendations, I suggest CliftonStrengths, Myers-Briggs, Enneagram, or Working Genius. Once you get the results from these tests, reflect on them and ask yourself whether you agree or disagree.
3. Commit to at least two actions you can take every day or week to refine your strengths. I suggest you choose something you enjoy.
4. Write what love means to you in relation to business and leadership. Does the concept of love feel uncomfortable for you?

Reflection and Looking Forward

This chapter covered three important steps you need to take to become the type of leader people want to follow. First, you must discover your true self. This process enables your purpose, vision, and strengths. Second, you must refine your strengths and use them to positively impact others. Finally, you must love people expecting nothing in return.

As you finish this chapter on the steps to becoming the type of leader people want to follow, it becomes clear that true leadership requires authenticity, originality, genuine confidence, and a commitment to love and serve others. But what does it mean to embark on this transformative journey?

In the next chapter, we delve into the benefits and price of becoming such a leader. We'll analyse the characteristics of outstanding leaders, their personal sacrifices, and the rewards and challenges of genuine leadership.

CHAPTER 8

THE BENEFITS AND PRICE OF BECOMING THE TYPE OF LEADER PEOPLE WANT TO FOLLOW

*If you help others get what they want,
you will always have what you need.*
~ Zig Ziglar

When you go through the three steps I described in earlier chapters, you begin a transformation into your true self. As someone who has experienced this, I want to share what you can expect.

The Premise

Leaders people want to follow will reap both rewards and costs in their journey.

Let's delve into the essence of true leadership and the qualities that make leaders exceptional and inspire others to follow them. These nine benefits of being a leader people want to follow are the key elements that set apart remarkable leaders from the rest.

These qualities, from authenticity and originality to genuine confidence and freedom from competition, create a powerful foundation for effective leadership. They pave the way for personal fulfilment, fearlessness, internal motivation and passion, high energy, and the attraction of both people and opportunities. By understanding and embodying these benefits, you can unlock your full leadership potential and become the type of leader others are naturally drawn to.

1. **Authenticity**. Authenticity means showing up as your true self and being comfortable in who you are. Leaders often wear a mask at work, pretending to be someone they're not. But true leadership cannot be achieved by imitating others. People follow relatable and authentic leaders. Authenticity is akin to humility—being grounded in your true essence. You can learn to be authentic by following the steps in Chapter 7.

2. **Originality**. Being original sets you apart from the crowd. It's unique and genuine qualities that distinguish great leaders from others, not necessarily their intelligence. Embracing your originality is essential to becoming the type of leader people want to follow. Discovering your unique value and

refining it will provide clarity in your purpose and enable you to contribute meaningfully. Remember, genuine value is recognised and rewarded.

3. **Genuine Confidence.** Genuine confidence comes from knowing and accepting yourself, loving who you are, and recognising your worth and contribution to the world. It is the perfect blend of self-assurance and humility. Genuine confidence allows you to be comfortable with your decisions, seek help when needed, take risks, and acknowledge your limitations. It is anchored in a deep sense of security and generates trust and inspiration among those you lead.

4. **Freedom from Competition and Comparison.** Becoming the type of leader people want to follow liberates you from the need to compete or compare yourself to others. Your success is not measured by how you measure up against others but by fulfilling your purpose and potential. Instead of perceiving others as obstacles or competitors, view them as collaborators and enablers on your journey. When you understand your uniqueness and focus on your vision, competition and comparison become irrelevant.

5. **Personal Fulfilment.** Personal fulfilment is not about your own achievements but about the joy and satisfaction that comes from helping others. It is derived from adding value and making a positive

impact in the lives of others. Your vision should be centred around contributing to humanity. When you fulfil that vision, you experience a profound sense of fulfilment. Ultimately, people remember leaders for how they positively impacted lives, not for material possessions or titles.

6. **Fearlessness.** True leaders are fearless, not because they lack fear, but because they triumph over it. Courage is born from acknowledging fear and acting despite it. Being bold allows you to step outside your comfort zone, take calculated risks, and inspire others to do the same. Fearlessness is a hallmark of effective leadership and propels you forward in the face of challenges.

7. **Internal Motivation and Passion.** Becoming the type of leader people want to follow ignites internal motivation and passion within you. True leadership is not dependent on external sources of motivation; it stems from a deep conviction and a sense of purpose. When your vision aligns with your values and beliefs, you are motivated to persevere, even amid adversity. Passion fuels your drive and sustains you through challenging times.

8. **High Energy.** Leaders who inspire others possess high energy. This means having the capacity to operate at a high level. Leadership can be demanding, and leaders often carry significant responsibilities. To maintain effectiveness, it is crucial to

manage pressure and remain calm. This requires a sense of self-security, a heart to serve others, and an optimistic outlook. When you possess these qualities, you exude high energy and remain unfazed by external circumstances.

9. **Attraction of People and Opportunities**. You become like a tree bearing fruit when you discover and refine your strengths. True leaders never seek followers; followers are attracted to them. Your strengths act as the fruit that draws people towards you. By becoming the type of leader people want to follow, you naturally attract like-minded individuals and opportunities that align with your purpose.

The Premise

There is a price to become the type of leader people want to follow

My Story

When I was in my early thirties, I tried for several years to lose weight and develop a muscular physique. I made many attempts and tried many fad diets. Honestly, I was kidding myself, as I was not following some basic laws of weight loss and building muscle.

I did a lot of reading to improve my knowledge. One of the key things I learned was that achieving my goals was possible, but required a lot of discipline. There was a well-known formula. There were good reasons I couldn't achieve my goals. With two young kids, a job that required lots of travel, and a penchant for junk food, I had my hands full. I had to follow a strict diet and do weight training at the gym three times a week to achieve my goal. Just two things, simple.

Some serious sacrifices were necessary to do this. First, I had to eat differently from the rest of the family. I had to buy specific foods, eat at different times of the day, and spend more on food. This was painful, as I sometimes felt bad not eating the same food as the family.

I turned down several opportunities to eat out with friends and family. When I had to eat out, I was conscientious about what I ate and always had the odd meal at the table.

Second, I sacrificed work and time at home to go to the gym regularly. Going to the gym disrupted my work pattern, which meant I had to leave work at a certain time. Because I had set times to visit the gym, which could take two hours overall, I could not help at home at certain times.

I felt guilty making changes that seemed selfish and could affect my family and work. I had to believe the sacrifice was for a greater cause. It was, indeed. Taking care of my health was important to ensure I could be there for my family and perform well at work. Ultimately, it was the case, as I achieved my weight and muscular goals, which improved my health and helped me perform better at work.

To become the type of leader people want to follow, understand that leadership comes at a personal cost. It requires sacrifice, humility, and a commitment to a higher cause. True leadership is not about personal gain or recognition, but about serving others. It involves taking responsibility for both failures and successes.

Leadership demands sacrifices. It can be costly. The question is not whether there is a price to pay, because there is; but whether you are willing to pay it. Just as a diamond is refined to become valuable, your journey to becoming a great leader will require personal refining. It is crucial to keep the end goal in mind and recognise that the beneficiaries of your sacrifices are often others. Your commitment to a greater cause will transform you and enable you to reach your maximum potential.

Great leadership indeed comes at a personal cost, and several key aspects contribute to this cost.

1. **Price to become more valuable**: Becoming a great leader requires continuous growth and development. It involves investing time and effort into enhancing one's knowledge, skills, and abilities. This may mean attending trainings, seeking mentorship, or pursuing further education. It requires a commitment to personal improvement and a willingness to invest in oneself.

2. **Price to get out of your comfort zone:** Effective leaders will step outside of their comfort zones and take risks. They understand that growth and progress often lie beyond familiar territory. This may involve embracing new challenges, facing fears, and pushing oneself beyond perceived limits. It requires

courage and a willingness to embrace discomfort for the sake of personal and professional growth.

3. **Price to take on responsibility and be accountable for one's own actions**: Great leaders take ownership of their decisions and actions. They understand that leadership entails responsibility and accountability. This means accepting the consequences of their choices, admitting mistakes, and learning from failures. It requires humility and the willingness to learn and grow from setbacks.

4. **Price to take on the responsibility and be accountable for others:** Alongside personal responsibility, leaders also take on the responsibility of guiding and supporting their team or organisation. They prioritise the needs and well-being of others, sometimes at the expense of their own interests. This may involve making tough decisions, advocating for their team, and ensuring the success of those they lead. It requires selflessness and a commitment to serving others.

5. **Price of personal sacrifice**: Leadership often involves sacrificing personal desires and priorities for the greater good. Leaders may need to dedicate more time, energy, and resources to their roles, sometimes at the expense of personal pursuits. It requires a willingness to make sacrifices and prioritise the team's or organisation's needs over individual needs.

6. **Price of setbacks, failures, and criticism**: Leaders are not immune to setbacks, failures, or criticism. In fact, they may face heightened scrutiny and personal attacks because of their leadership positions. This can be challenging, and may require resilience and perseverance. Leaders are human beings, like everyone else. They have emotions and can be hurt by others. Leaders must be able to navigate through adversity, learn from failures, and remain focused on their goals despite setbacks.

7. **Price of not being understood**: Leadership often involves making tough decisions and taking unconventional approaches. This can cause being misunderstood or facing resistance from others. Leaders may need to navigate through scepticism, opposition, or lack of support. It requires strong conviction in one's vision and the ability to communicate and inspire others, even in the face of resistance.

8. **Price of full transparency and vulnerability**: Effective leaders often show transparency and vulnerability. They are open about their thoughts, feelings, and challenges, creating an environment of trust and authenticity. Openness can be challenging, as it involves revealing vulnerabilities and difficulties.

9. **Price of unpopularity**: Don't become a leader if you want to be liked or popular with everyone. The price of leadership often includes the risk of

unpopularity. Leaders must make tough decisions and choices that may not always be well-received by everyone. They must have the courage to stand by their convictions and do what they believe is right, even if it means upsetting some people. Being liked is not the primary goal of leadership. Rather, it is about earning respect through integrity, fairness, and consistent decision-making.

Great leaders prioritise the long-term success and well-being of their organisation or team over short-term popularity, even if it means making decisions that are unpopular. They will face criticism and navigate through challenging situations, staying true to their values and vision. The price of unpopularity is an inherent part of leadership. Effective leaders are prepared to face it to fulfil their responsibilities.

ACTION PLAN

1. Are you a leader people want to follow? Rate yourself from 1 to 10, with 10 being the highest. If you are not in a leadership position, pick a leader you know well and answer these questions about that person.
2. Review the nine benefits you've received by being a leader people want to follow, and list all that you possess.
3. Review the nine prices you've had to pay by being a leader people want to follow.

CHAPTER 8

Reflection and Looking Forward

True leadership comes with a cost. It involves personal growth, discomfort, responsibility, sacrifice, setbacks, criticism, resistance, transparency, and vulnerability. Despite the cost, the rewards of leadership, such as personal growth, making a positive impact, and influencing others, make it a worthy and fulfilling journey.

In the next and final chapter, we will explore the powerful concept of gratitude and how it emerges as a transformative element for effective leaders. Cultivating gratitude increases trust and cooperation. Showing gratitude can recognise and appreciate others, create a positive work atmosphere, and motivate employees.

By expressing gratitude, leaders can inspire loyalty, boost morale, and create an environment where individuals feel valued and supported. Gratitude allows leaders to develop a growth mindset, enabling them to learn from setbacks and seek opportunities for improvement. Gratitude is essential for true leadership, enabling leaders to maximise their teams' potential and create a positive organisational culture.

CHAPTER 9

THE POWER AND BENEFIT OF GRATITUDE

Whatever you appreciate, appreciates.
- John C. Maxwell

The Story of "The Power of Thank-You."

Once upon a time, a wise old man lived in a small village. He was known for his kindness, wisdom, and gratitude. One day, a young boy approached the old man seeking advice.

The boy said, "Old man, I feel unappreciated and unnoticed by others. I do my best, but it seems like no one cares. What should I do?"

The wise old man smiled and said, "My young friend, I will tell you a story. There was once a farmer who had a loyal and hardworking horse. The horse helped him with all his tasks on the farm, ploughing the fields, carrying heavy loads,

True Leadership

and more. The farmer appreciated the horse's efforts but never expressed it.

"One day, a neighbouring farmer visited and noticed the horse's strength and obedience. He said to the farmer, 'You have a remarkable horse. It's clear that your horse is a treasure.' The farmer nodded but remained silent.

"The neighbouring farmer continued, 'You know, it would be a shame if your horse were to leave you and come to work for me. I would value and appreciate such a fine creature.' Hearing this, the farmer realised the importance of expressing gratitude.

"The next morning, the farmer went to his horse, patted it gently, and said, 'Thank you for your hard work. I appreciate everything you do for me.' The horse's eyes gleamed with joy and determination.

"In the following days, the farmer continued to express his gratitude. He would talk to the horse, share kind words, and acknowledge its efforts. The horse grew happier and more devoted.

"As time went on, the neighbouring farmer visited again. To his surprise, the horse refused to leave the farmer's side. It had become loyal and dedicated, not only because of its abilities, but also because of the appreciation it received."

The wise old man concluded, "My young friend, the story teaches us the power of appreciation. When we express gratitude and acknowledge the efforts of others, it creates a bond of loyalty, motivation, and happiness. People thrive when they feel valued and appreciated. So, remember to always say thank you and show appreciation to those around you."

CHAPTER 9

The young boy listened attentively and left with a newfound understanding of the importance of appreciation in fostering positive relationships and creating a harmonious community.

The Premise

Gratefulness is showing appreciation to others for what they have done for us.

I cannot overstate the importance and criticality of gratitude in becoming the type of leader people want to follow. In my personal journey as a leader, I have found that expressing gratitude has been beneficial not only for me, but also for others. Expressing gratitude positively impacts us personally, as it changes our perspective on life and how we lead. For others, receiving gratitude makes them feel valued and appreciated.

Here are some important reasons expressing gratitude to others is critical.

1. **It humbles us**: Gratitude helps us understand that most of our achievements result from the contributions of others. It helps us focus on the support and contributions of the people around us. You couldn't have achieved your recent leadership success without the help of others. As C. S. Lewis states, humility is not thinking less of yourself; it is thinking of yourself less. When we practice expressing gratitude, we think of ourselves less.

   People appreciate humility in leaders. Some leaders worry expressing gratitude may make them appear weaker. I have been there myself. I have sometimes felt the need to focus on my own contributions and give less attention to others in order to demonstrate my value. However, I have learned over time that this only alienates people and does not reflect reality. As John Maxwell says, "You are never as good as people say you are and never as bad as you think you are."

2. **Fosters positive relationships**: Gratitude helps build and maintain positive relationships with others. When leaders express gratitude for their team members' contributions, it creates a sense of value and recognition. This strengthens the bond between leaders and their teams.

3. **Inspires loyalty and commitment:** When leaders show gratitude, it creates a sense of loyalty and commitment among their team members. Recognising and appreciating their efforts and accomplishments makes employees feel valued and motivated to go the extra mile. Gratitude helps cultivate a culture of trust and loyalty within the organisation.

I cannot recount the number of times I have expressed gratitude to people for simply doing their jobs, and they have helped me. I remember one Christmas holiday when my boss had a critical piece of work she wanted to deliver. She wanted my team's support, even during our holiday time with family. Saying no would have been understandable.

However, I realised how important this task was to my boss. I felt a loyalty and commitment to her, so I said yes. I also got the commitment from my team. My boss is someone who always expressed gratitude to me, and I felt valued. Therefore, I was prepared to sacrifice for her in her time of need.

4. **Increases resilience**: Gratitude promotes resilience in leaders. Leaders can maintain a positive mindset even in challenging situations by focusing on what they are grateful for. This positivity allows them to navigate obstacles with resilience, inspiring their teams to do the same.

5. **Cultivates a culture of appreciation**: Gratitude sets the tone for a culture of appreciation within an organisation. When leaders express gratitude, it encourages others to do the same. This creates a positive feedback loop where team members recognise and appreciate each other's efforts. This leads to a supportive and engaged work environment.

6. **Improves overall health and well-being**: Gratitude has many benefits for personal well-being. It reduces stress and improves mental health. When leaders prioritise their own well-being and express gratitude, they set an example for their teams to do the same. I'm sure most leaders have experienced the burden of leadership. We feel the need to make things happen, to achieve our goals and win. Sometimes we can take things too personally and

shoulder all the weight of the role. This is wrong, and will certainly have a negative impact on our mental well-being. When we develop a habit of expressing gratitude, we create a culture where people will take ownership and help reduce the burden on leaders. Expressing gratitude reminds us that other people are with us and are there to help us. It helps reduce the pressure on us and share it among the team. This significantly improves our mental and physical well-being.

7. **Enables us to give back**: When we express gratitude regularly, it shows us how lucky and privileged we are. Leaders aren't always the smartest, most experienced, or talented in the room. When we appreciate how lucky we are to be in our position, we are compelled to give back to others. This could include mentoring, financial aid, and advocating for others.

Ken Frazier's Story

Ken Frazier, former CEO of Merck, a Fortune 500 company in the United States, is a great example of this. Ken was one of the very few African American CEOs in Fortune 500. He was born in a very poor part of the US. His father was a janitor, and his mother died when he was twelve. Even after

CHAPTER 9

reaching the pinnacle of success, fate chose him for something that infused the purpose of his life.

Ken was chosen to be a part of the ground-breaking social integration project in his home city, Philadelphia. The educational initiative sought to bridge the racial divide in the city. It bussed several African-American kids from their homes to a faraway top-performing school. Ken was one of the few African-American participants. This project transformed Ken's life, giving him a platform to advocate for racial equality. The project's collaboration and diverse perspectives inspired him to become an advocate for social justice in his community.

Frazier is renowned for his exceptional leadership skills and commitment to community engagement. As CEO of Merck, Ken consistently showed the importance of giving back to society. He did this through philanthropic efforts and his deep appreciation for the communities in which Merck operates. He fostered a culture of gratitude, encouraging employees to appreciate each other's contributions. Frazier's commitment to corporate social responsibility and community projects made a lasting impression on the company. Ken Frazier's success stems from his exceptional leadership and genuine commitment to giving back to the community.

Expressing gratitude is critical in being an authentic leader. It builds positive relationships, strengthens emotional intelligence, creates loyalty, increases resilience, shows appreciation, and increases well-being. Gratitude is a powerful tool that leaders can use to create a positive and impactful leadership style.

The Premise

How do I express gratitude in my life?

I am grateful for my faith.

Faith is the cornerstone of my life and my number one priority above anything else. I understand that not everyone shares my faith or its importance, and that's okay. My faith has shaped many of my values and perspectives about people and life. The Bible is central to my faith and provides me with leadership principles that continuously benefit me. Many secular leadership principles are rooted in the Bible, making faith and secular leadership compatible. Expressing the importance of my faith to my colleagues has never been an issue for me. In fact, it has been positively received. I am grateful to my parents for raising me with faith and allowing me to explore it myself. My faith has been the biggest contributor to who I am today, providing me with purpose, peace, and inner security.

I am grateful for the opportunity to discover my true self.

I am grateful for the opportunity to discover my true self. Over the past 20 years, every day I wake up and thank God for the person I have become. I am acutely aware of who I was over two decades ago and who I am now. During this time, I have discovered my true identity and am content with who I am. This self-discovery has provided me with incredible inner security and peace. Many factors have contributed to shaping the person I am today, and I am grateful for the opportunities I have had. I have encountered many individuals who live in fear, feel insecure, and lack inner peace. I believe their struggles stem from not discovering their authentic selves. As I mentioned earlier in this book, when you uncover your true identity, it changes everything.

I am grateful for the challenges and crises I have faced.

I'm grateful for the crises and challenges I've faced. This may surprise some of you, as you may wonder why I am thankful for negative experiences. Frankly, I wouldn't be where I am today if I hadn't gone through what I have. My self-discovery journey began at sixteen during my first major personal crisis. It solidified my faith in myself.

Throughout my life, I have faced several other significant challenges related to family, friends, and my career. I have faced relationship difficulties, experienced job loss, and been uncertain about the future. I am grateful that I could overcome these challenges. I am grateful for the lessons I learned from these situations. They allowed me to see different perspectives and provided opportunities for growth.

As a result, I emerged from these situations as a changed and better person. While the core of who I am remained the same, these experiences helped remove many impurities and flaws within me. I recognise I still have many areas for improvement, and I am open to future opportunities for personal refinement.

I am grateful for my upbringing.

I am grateful for my family's upbringing. My parents did a great job raising me and I appreciate it. While they were far from perfect, they instilled critical values in me that have shaped who I am today. They also worked tirelessly to provide my siblings and me with the best education. My father remains a mentor to me. He embodies the qualities of an authentic leader, which aligns with the essence of this book. I only fully appreciated my father once I started living my life, working, getting married, and having children.

As for my mother, she showered me with love and care despite the challenges she faced herself. She was always there for me, a loyal friend who made my upbringing enjoyable. Her incredible generosity and charitable nature are qualities I admire. I consider myself extremely lucky and blessed to have been raised by both of them.

I am also grateful for my siblings. They have always been supportive during the difficult moments of my life. They have shown me great generosity and love frequently. Despite not speaking daily or knowing every detail of their lives, I share a unique bond with my siblings. We have never experienced sibling rivalries or animosities, which I know can be common in other families. I mention this because I've heard stories about such dynamics.

CHAPTER 9

I am grateful to my wife.

I am grateful to my wife. The reason I married her was because I believed she would help me fulfil my purpose in life. Before getting married, I clearly understood my purpose and vision. I viewed major decisions through my purpose and evaluated if a potential partner would support my goals. On our first date, I strongly sensed that she was the right person for me. We connected on a deep level, both entering the relationship with a clear sense of our individual purposes.

My wife has been an incredible blessing to my career. When we married, I was still a PhD student with limited financial resources and uncertain prospects. Not everyone would have taken a chance on me, but she believed in my ambitious dreams and visions. She believed in me when few did, and still does.

Now, fifteen years later, I have achieved significant milestones in my career and she has been by my side throughout the journey. She has made sacrifices in her own career and personal life to ensure my success. I am grateful because my career would not have reached its current heights without her unwavering support.

I am grateful for the opportunities I have been given.

I am grateful for the opportunities I have been given. This holds great significance for me. Despite my lack of experience, I have been fortunate to be granted many career opportunities. People often believed in me and gave me a chance.

Reflecting on my journey, starting from my university education, I realise the doors that opened for me. I attended the University of Edinburgh for a prestigious joint degree in Electrical and Mechanical Engineering. Most individuals who applied also had impeccable grades. However, I was admitted. You may say I deserved it, but I am certain there were others who deserved it just as much. A similar situation occurred when I started my PhD without a master's degree, despite most others having one.

Shortly after completing my PhD, I received what I consider the biggest opportunity in my career. This marked the beginning of my leadership journey in the corporate world. It was the dream job I mentioned earlier in this book.

Later, I was headhunted for another executive director role at a different large organisation. Throughout my career, I have been given or been promoted to roles in which I had no prior experience. The common thread in these situations was that people believed in me and had confidence in my ability to learn and excel.

It hasn't always been smooth sailing in these roles. At the time of writing this book, I was encouraged to transition to a sales role. I had no prior experience in sales. However, the leader I now report to believed in me and gave me the opportunity. I am now grateful for all these diverse experiences as I believe they are shaping me to become a better leader and person.

I am thankful to the several individuals who believed in me, particularly Michael and Roger, who gave me opportunities to work in executive roles. I am also grateful to Justo, Taira, Tom, Eric, and Thomas, all of whom took a chance on me. Their reasons may always be a mystery to me, but I still feel thankful toward them. Without their support and belief in me, I would not be where I am today.

I am grateful for the critical feedback I receive.

I am a firm believer in soliciting feedback, particularly critical feedback. I believe it is a way to become more self-aware, understand how I impact others, and discover new growth opportunities. Every few years, I conduct an anonymous 360-degree feedback process. This allows me to gather feedback from a wide range of people at different levels, from several teams, and from various perspectives. Each time I have done this, I have received valuable, encouraging, and challenging feedback. It's uncomfortable to seek feedback, especially when there is a fear of receiving negative comments. Thus, I understand why some people may choose not to pursue this route.

My Story

Besides formal 360-degree feedback, I also encourage people to share feedback with me in our conversations. I remember one instance when I spoke to a senior executive in my company after returning from a trip to Brazil together. The executive had taken me to Brazil to attend and contribute to an important meeting. The executive was dissatisfied with my behaviour in the meeting. According to the executive, I appeared quiet and aloof. Initially, I was surprised to hear this feedback.

Upon reflection, I realised the executive was right. I sometimes come across as aloof in meetings. Not because I am uninterested, but because my natural inclination is to observe, listen, and only speak when I have something important to contribute. I have learned others can perceive this differently. This feedback from a senior leader in my company was certainly a wake-up call for me. I am grateful for it. I thanked the executive for sharing their perspective and promised to make a change.

Receiving feedback like this is invaluable to me as it allows me to grow and improve as a person and a leader. At the very least, it will enable me to be self-aware. It requires humility and a willingness to acknowledge areas where I can develop further. I am grateful for those who provide me with feedback, as it helps me become a better version of myself.

I am grateful to my mentors.

I am grateful to my mentors. I appreciate the knowledge and guidance I receive from the mentors in my life and career. I have both direct and indirect mentors. Direct mentors are individuals I engage with on a one-on-one basis, while indirect mentors are those who mentor me through programs or books. In both cases, I carefully choose my mentors. I select mentors who share my values and whom I respect. My mentors are the source of my most valuable leadership knowledge.

One of my indirect mentors is Myles Munroe, a highly regarded expert on leadership. I have taken part in his mentorship program, read all his books, and listened to most of his teachings. He has had a significant impact on my journey of discovering my purpose and becoming the leader I am today. I also have other mentors, including my father, Igbuan, Sarah, and Mike. Everyone has positively influenced me in different ways, and I am grateful to them.

I am grateful to the many authors who have impacted me.

Many authors have deeply influenced me, and I am grateful. I cannot speak highly enough of books. I consider myself a serial reader, and I believe that books have the power to change lives. It still amazes me how affordable books are today, considering the immense impact they can have on people. I have read many books, particularly on leadership, from which I have gained a wealth of knowledge. These books have taught me principles and skills that have improved me as a person and made me a better leader. Besides books, I would also include podcasts as an important source of knowledge. I am an avid listener of relevant podcasts that provide valuable insights.

I want to express my sincere gratitude to all the authors who have had the courage to share their thoughts and ideas. I cannot list all the authors, but am grateful to each one of them.

There is one author, Chandler Bolt, the author of *Published*, whom I would like to highlight. He is the reason this book has been published and why you are reading it. In his book and podcasts, he encourages aspiring writers to focus on writing for just one person who needs their help.

In writing this book, I struggled to come to terms with it. I felt I had nothing new to say about leadership, and everyone already knew what I wanted to share. Because of Chandler's perspective, I shifted my mindset and realised that there is at least one person out there who will find my book helpful. Hopefully, many more individuals will benefit from it.

ACTION PLAN

I hope this chapter has helped you reflect on gratitude and the people who have contributed to your success. To make gratitude a practical part of your life, I recommend the following action plan.

1. Identify five important areas of your life, such as family, job, health, relationships, etc.
2. For each of the five areas, write down ten things for which you are grateful. With each item, identify a named person who has played a role in helping you achieve or appreciate that aspect of your life.
3. Purchase or create a gratitude journal. This can be a physical journal or an online journal. Every evening, take a few moments to write at least three things you are grateful for from that day.
4. Make it a daily practice to express gratitude to at least one person. It can be a simple thank-you note, a genuine compliment, or an act of kindness. Show appreciation to someone who has made a positive impact on your life.

CHAPTER 9

By implementing these four steps, you can cultivate gratitude in your life and acknowledge the contributions of others. This practice will enhance your overall well-being and strengthen your relationships.

EPILOGUE
Call to Action

Reflect on the lessons learned, growth experienced, and the journey ahead as you conclude this transformative book on true leadership. Throughout the chapters, you have explored several principles and practices that can transform you into the type of leader people want to follow.

You now have the knowledge to embrace your true leadership potential. Remember that leadership is not an endpoint, but an ongoing journey of growth, learning, and adaptation. It is a commitment to continuous self-discovery, refining your gifts and loving people.

As you move forward, keep these key takeaways in mind.

Vision and Purpose: Your vision and purpose as a leader provide the guiding light for your actions and inspire those around you. Continually refine and communicate your vision, aligning it with your team's and organisation's evolving needs.

Character and Integrity: Uphold the highest standards of character and integrity in your leadership journey. Act with honesty, authenticity, and fairness, setting a positive example for others to follow. Character will protect your success.

Self-Development and Awareness: Cultivate self-awareness and a growth mindset. Continuously seek opportunities for personal and professional development, embracing feedback and learning from both successes and failures.

Communication and Collaboration: Master the art of effective communication, actively listening, and fostering open dialogue. Embrace collaboration, harnessing your team's collective strengths and diversity to drive innovation and achieve shared goals.

Empathy and Empowerment: Lead with empathy, understanding the unique needs and perspectives of those you lead. Empower others by providing support, opportunities for growth, and a safe environment where everyone's voice is heard and valued.

Resilience and Adaptability: Embrace change and navigate challenges with resilience and adaptability. Embrace a mindset of continuous improvement, embracing new ideas, technologies, and strategies to stay ahead in an ever-changing world.

Gratitude and Appreciation: Remember the power of gratitude and appreciation in your leadership journey. Express genuine gratitude to those who contribute to your success, fostering a positive and supportive work environment.

Epilogue

As you embark on your continued leadership journey, remember that true leadership is not about personal glory or titles. It is about making a positive impact, uplifting those around you, and leaving a legacy. Each day presents new opportunities to inspire, influence, and empower others.

Take the knowledge and insights from this book and apply them with intention and purpose. Embrace challenges as opportunities for growth and transformation. Lead with authenticity, empathy, and a genuine desire to serve others.

Your journey as a true leader has only just begun. Embrace it with passion, courage, and unwavering determination. The world needs leaders like you—leaders who can make a profound difference in the lives of individuals, teams, and organisations.

Congratulations on embarking on this transformative path of true leadership. The future awaits, and it is yours to shape.

ACKNOWLEDGEMENTS

First and foremost, I want to say an enormous thank you to my wife, Ebiere, and my two boys, Noah and Emeka. This book would not have been completed without their support and encouragement. I would also like to thank Taira Hall and Ben Topliss for allowing me to share the original ideas of this book in a public setting. This encouraged me to persevere and complete my book. Thank you also to Michael Arumemi-Ikhide and Roger Whittle for believing in me and giving me opportunities that have changed my life. Finally, thank you to all my extended family and friends who have encouraged me and kept me accountable in this literary journey.

ABOUT THE AUTHOR

Gabriel Bolu is a seasoned senior strategy professional with over 15 years of experience in solving complex problems through strategic thinking and collaboration. Gabriel has worked in a senior management roles across a wide  range of industries, spanning Aerospace Engineering, Air Transportation, Construction, Legal and Financial Services. Based in the United Kingdom, Gabriel has a proven track record of driving organisational success and achieving remarkable results.

With a strong educational background, Gabriel holds an MSc in Air Transport Management from Cranfield University, an Engineering Doctorate (PhD) in Non-destructive Evaluation from the University of Strathclyde, and a BEng in Electrical & Mechanical Engineering from the University of Edinburgh.

Beyond his professional achievements, Gabriel is a dedicated individual with a passion for leadership and helping people maximise their potential. Gabriel has worked with and being mentored by some of the world's experts on Leadership, such as Dr Myles Munroe. With his extensive experience and expertise in leadership, Gabriel Bolu's book on "True Leadership: How to Become the Type of Leader People Want to Follow" promises to provide valuable insights and guidance for aspiring leaders seeking to become an authentic leader that makes a positive impact in their organisations and beyond.

Review Ask

URGENT PLEA!

Thank You For Reading My Book!
I really appreciate all of your feedback and
I love hearing what you have to say.

I need your input to make the next version of this
book and my future books better.

Please take two minutes now to leave a helpful review on Amazon letting me know what you thought of the book:
https://rebrand.ly/crdywcu

Thanks so much!
- Dr Gabriel Bolu

Printed in Great Britain
by Amazon

27901134R00104